Partners for Special Needs

Learn how to collaborate with parents and special education advocates to ensure student success. This practical book shows you how to navigate the tricky path to meeting special education goals and outcomes. It also provides strategies to help you communicate and partner more effectively with families and specialists.

Part I of the book offers key information on how special education has evolved over recent decades and what the Individualized Education Plan process entails. Part II features techniques for strengthening communication so you can avoid conflict and create as strong a partnership as possible. You'll learn the specific roles of advocates and parents, and you'll gain practical strategies for communicating proactively and managing communication breakdowns. You'll also uncover how to overcome the challenges of working with people during difficult times.

The book is filled with tips, examples, and reflection questions to help you implement the ideas immediately. With the essential strategies in this book, you can become the best support system for the child or children you serve!

Douglas J. Fiore is the author of eight books for educators, including *School-Community Relations* and *Dealing with Difficult Parents*, written with Todd Whitaker. Doug has served as a teacher, a principal, a professor, and a consultant, and he most recently served as a provost and vice president for academic affairs.

Julie Anne Fiore has been an educator for thirteen years, spending her most recent year as an Inclusion Intervention Specialist for middle school students. A proponent of partnerships, she insists that teachers engage students, parents, guardians, and those they hire in ensuring student success.

T0341244

Partners for Special Needs

How Teachers Can Effectively Collaborate with Parents and Other Advocates

Douglas J. Fiore and Julie Anne Fiore

Routledge
Taylor & Francis Group

NEW YORK AND LONDON

First published 2018
by Routledge
711 Third Avenue, New York, NY 10017

and by Routledge
2 Park Square, Milton Park, Abingdon, Oxon, OX14 4RN

Routledge is an imprint of the Taylor & Francis Group, an informa business

Library of Congress Cataloging-in-Publication Data
A catalog record for this book has been requested

ISBN: 978-1-138-71470-0 (hbk)
ISBN: 978-1-138-71473-1 (pbk)
ISBN: 978-1-315-22915-7 (ebk)

Typeset in Palatino
by Keystroke, Neville Lodge, Tettenhall, Wolverhampton

Contents

About the Authors

Dr. Douglas and Mrs. Julie Fiore have a combined 47 years of service in various sectors of education. In those 47 combined years, their collective service has been in the roles of paraprofessional, teacher, principal, professor, dean, provost, and state education department official. They have consulted with countless schools and districts, educators and researchers, and have written other books for educators. Doug and Julie are frequent presenters at state, regional, and national conferences in the field of education.

While Julie's expertise is in everything related to special education, instructional design, differentiation, and co-teaching, Doug's expertise is in communication, relationship building, and leadership. Doug has a Ph.D. in Educational Administration from Indiana State University, and one of his textbooks, *School-Community Relations*, is a bestseller in its field. He is also co-author of the top-selling *Dealing with Difficult Parents, 2nd Edition*, and *A School Leader's Guide to Dealing with Difficult Parents*, co-written with Todd Whitaker. Julie has degrees from the University of Akron and Western Governors University.

Preface

Our combined experiences in K-12 education (along with the collaborative professional partnerships we've established from all around the country) have given us both opportunities to vet information which we feel that today's educators and parents need and will use in both regular education settings and special education settings. No matter where we go, or how much we learn about the experiences educators and families have, very little information exists that can help teachers or administrators understand how to successfully navigate the crucial processes that exist in the planning, assessing, and discussion of special education goals, behaviors, and outcomes. It seems that now, more than ever, more information is needed to ensure the success of all students in the classroom. It is a litigious time in education. It is always important to be over-prepared rather than under-prepared regarding the finer details of special education legislation and the implications resulting from that legislation. It is apparent that special education teachers, through their postsecondary preparation and/or through their experiences, have learned how to collaborate with parents of children with special needs and with advocates who, oftentimes, are hired by parents to help ensure that their child's academic goals are appropriate and their needs are met. However, there appears to be a dearth of training for other teachers, staff members, and administrators. As our experiences have shown us, collaborations, particularly in special education settings, are not an area in which many educators receive professional development. These experiences have led us, in many ways, to conceiving and writing this book.

Our purpose here is twofold. First, we want to help everybody understand how crucial the relationships between teachers, parents, and advocates are to success for children with special needs. We want to ensure that everybody is on the same page in their understanding of the special education process, and we really hope that all parties can approach any Individualized Education Plan meetings or other conferences about student learning with similar goals and expectations. Part I of this book provides information on how special education has evolved over recent decades, due largely to legislation and legal challenges. We also want to ensure that all readers are knowledgeable about the Universal Design for Learning and the Individualized Education Plan process.

Second, we want to help strengthen communication. In our experiences, communication breakdowns and barriers account for a great deal of conflict in special education meetings and other situations. We want to help ensure that teachers, parents, and advocates know how best to communicate with each other to ensure that their partnership is as strong as possible. We intend to be a resource for those times when a conversation or face-to-face meeting is making each party nervous. We wrote Part II with this purpose in mind. In Part II, we explain the specific roles of advocates and parents, and we provide you with important information on the communication process, communication breakdowns, and the challenges of working with people during difficult times.

Both of us believe that adult partnerships lead to student success. We are teachers, parents, and advocates. We are on the same journey as you. Our goal is simply to make that journey easier and more productive for the benefit of you and the children you serve. Thank you for reading and using what has been the culmination of years of observation, intense research, and dedicated application to the art and science of teaching. We hope it motivates and inspires you to be the best support system you can be for the child or children you serve.

Douglas and Julie Fiore

Part I

The Practice of Special Education

1

The Development of Special Education Practices

Throughout this chapter, we set the stage for the current, contemporary notion of special education, best methods for educating students with special needs, and legal challenges that may be yet to come. By illustrating some of the most significant changes to happen in special education practices and advocacy over the past half century, we can best understand how we got to where we are today in special education.

Historically, teachers educated students in classrooms where learners were more alike than they were different. In the early 1970s, 1980s, and 1990s most instruction was developed and implemented according to grade level, age, and ability. Other considerations may have included arranging students according to sex or particular interest. The result of these homogeneous groupings meant that the planning and focus of student learning was more aligned with the teacher and the whole group rather than the individual learner. The "outliers", specifically students with exceptional learning needs, typically were forced to mold to the majority. This practice of educating students as a group often prevented the "outliers" from developing to reach their potential. Thus, the gifted student and the special needs student rarely worked within what Lev Vygotsky (the Soviet psychologist and founder of cultural-historical psychology) coined as the "Zone of Proximal Development", meaning where learning is not too challenging or too easy, but right at the student's appropriate level, which enabled the student to learn independently, with minimal support. Students falling outside the norm were typically considered educational afterthoughts. The gifted student was given more work – not necessarily challenging work, but a greater amount – while the special needs student was given less work or alternative activities like coloring or listening to music, because the work was "just too hard". Teachers often worked independently: planning lessons, implementing instruction, and grading work. Teaching was, at times, a lonely profession. The collaborative aspect of teaching occurred after instruction ended: at staff meetings, parent–teacher conferences, and at the occasional evening event planned for families for mostly fundraising purposes. These after-instruction events were often where teachers worked with colleagues and parents to "sort out" problems in the classroom. This left teachers and parents feeling like "islands", alone in their perspective of the student/child.

Naturally, over time, evidence of this type of educational system showed that teachers and parents were not focused on working as collaborative team partners, but as competitors in a race to see who would "win" at making sure the child's needs were met. Oftentimes, teachers felt that parents didn't care about students, and parents felt the same way about teachers. This did nothing to promote a sense of community, nor did it help foster a rapport between the school and the family. These ills that occurred over time are prevalent in many schools today.

Special education advocacy or support for those with disabilities developed as a result of the Individuals with Disabilities Education Act (IDEA), which was reauthorized by the US Congress in 2004. (Further information about IDEA can be found in the Appendix.) Both parents and teachers found the laws and mandates of IDEA and the procedural implications for following IDEA to be incredibly complex. As a result, there was often a need for a third-party neutral interpreter to listen to the desire of both the parent and the teacher and to help find a workable solution that met the requirements of the law, but also demonstrated compassion for the child in his/her learning environment. Today, advocates for students with disabilities come from all walks of life. Some are former attorneys, while others are former teachers. Many refer to themselves as "educational consultants" and charge a fee for working with a family. Some attorneys do work for their clients "pro bono".

Advocacy has developed quite a bit since the 1970s, and legal challenges and interpretations are large parts of the reason why. Since special education regulations were often designed and written with little clarity, it has taken some big legal challenges, many ultimately heard by the United States Supreme Court, to more clearly define what the parameters are for educating students with special needs. Furthermore, it has taken the work and research of advocates to assure that procedures and policies are being followed in the best interests of the students they serve.

The Legal Environment

Never intended to be a "legal" environment, education in the latter part of the previous century was steeped in litigation. It began because of a sincere desire on the part of all teachers, parents, and community members to meet the needs of all learners. That, as we all know, is easier said than done in all cases.

Although our intention with this book is to help educators collaboratively work with parents and advocates so that all children receive the best education possible, it is unwise to ignore the legal parameters that govern our ability to do so. Oftentimes, we think of the law as something that describes minimums, regulations, and standards. Many educators get turned off by these discussions because they feel as though most teachers go far above and beyond what it is that they are "supposed to do". Nevertheless, we must acknowledge that much of the behavior governing education for students with special needs has its roots in legal standards. These standards of care have arisen because of things that were *not* being done for children in schools. These legal decisions only came about because students were *not* having their rights met by their teacher or their public school district.

What follow are summaries of six highly significant legal cases spanning a period of more than twenty years from the early 1980s through the early 2000s. It was during this period that many of the legal requirements placed on public schools and the legal rights of students that are taken for granted in most schools today were born. These six cases also gave rise to many acronyms, such as FAPE (free appropriate public education), that we regularly use in special education conversations today.

1. *Board of Education* v. *Rowley* (1982)

The decision in this US Supreme Court case set the standard and the baseline for many cases that have followed and really helped to frame the discussion about what schools were required to do relative to assuring a free appropriate public education (FAPE) for all students.

In a New York school district, prior to the 1976–1977 school year, parents Clifford and Nancy Rowley met with the principal of Furnace Woods Elementary School to discuss accommodations for their hearing-impaired daughter, Amy Rowley, who would be starting kindergarten there the following year. Amy was placed in a regular kindergarten class and was provided with a hearing aid. After a successful kindergarten year, Amy was promoted to first grade. An Individualized Education Plan (IEP) was created for Amy which included the continued use of her hearing aid. However, Amy's parents also wanted the school to provide a sign language interpreter. The school, in consultation with the district's Committee on the Handicapped, contended that Amy did not need an interpreter. They stated that Amy was achieving educationally and socially without the interpreter. The parents disagreed, and after several lower court rulings, the case made it all the way to the US Supreme Court. Before the Supreme Court decision, the parents had won at each level and the school was being chastised for not providing an interpreter.

On June 28, 1982 the court handed down a 6–3 decision which helped determine what is meant by FAPE. The decision, written by Justice William Rehnquist, stated that the purpose of IDEA was not to allow each child to achieve their full potential, but to simply provide sufficient resources for handicapped children to access education. Without the interpreter, the court reasoned, Amy did not have the same access to the curriculum as other students had. While the interpreter would not make Amy's educational experience optimal, it was considered a necessary accommodation to ensure that Amy was provided sufficient resources to, at least, access education.

The *Rowley* case has been cited by more than 3,000 court cases since 1982 that involved questions of a student's educational rights under IDEA.

2. Irving Independent School District v. Tatro (1984)

This landmark case involves an 8-year-old girl who was born with a defect known as spina bifida. As a result of this condition, she suffered from orthopedic and speech impairments and a neurogenic bladder, which prevented her from emptying her bladder voluntarily. Consequently, she needed to be catheterized every few hours during the school day to avoid serious injury to her kidneys. To accomplish this, a procedure known as clean intermittent catheterization (CIC) was prescribed. CIC is a simple procedure that can be performed in a few minutes by a layperson with less than an hour's training. The Irving School District refused to require that a school nurse perform the CIC for the student. They claimed that, despite the fact that CIC could easily be performed by a layperson, the procedure was medical in nature and outside of a school's scope of responsibility to a student. Making it all the way to the US Supreme Court, this case stands out as the Supreme Court's first attempt to define the distinction between school supportive health services, which officials must provide under IDEA as related services identified in students' IEPs if they are necessary to assist children with disabilities to benefit from special education, and medical services, which they are not required to supply unless they are for diagnostic or evaluative purposes. In determining that the school district was required to provide catheterization, the court stated that because this service was required in order for the student to remain at school during the day and because it was a simple procedure that could be performed easily by a layperson with less than an hour's training, it qualified for coverage under IDEA. This was a very significant decision, as it had been unclear where to draw the line with any services that appeared to be medical.

The court's differentiation between supportive health services and medical services stands today as the definition upon which decisions about medical care in schools are made.

3. School Committee of Town of Burlington, Massachusetts v. Department of Education of Massachusetts (1985)

This US Supreme Court cased focused on the rights parents have if they are dissatisfied with results of the IEP process under the (then) Education for All Handicapped Children Act (EHCA), now IDEA.

The case involved a family of a third grade student and the Burlington (Massachusetts) School District. The student's parents, believing that their child's learning disabilities were the result of serious neurological issues, disagreed with the level of services the school district proposed in the child's IEP. The school district based their IEP accommodations on their belief that the child was instead suffering from emotional issues and that additional accommodations were unnecessary. The dispute between the two parties continued throughout the school year, and the child continued to struggle under the school's IEP. During the constant debates on the merits of the IEP, the parents finally opted to remove the child from the public school and place him in a private school that better addressed his specific needs. The family then sought reimbursement from the school district for the cost of the private school fees because the school district had not provided the child with FAPE.

In the ultimate 9–0 ruling, the US Supreme Court determined that if a private school can be considered a proper placement, then school officials would have to create IEPs that permit students to attend the private schools and to reimburse their parents, retroactively. Furthermore, the court indicated that reimbursing parents was only paying what the school district would, or should, have spent in the first place had officials initially developed a proper IEP.

4. Honig v. Doe (1988)

Another case that reached the US Supreme Court and has had a dramatic impact on how schools discipline students with special needs is *Honig* v. *Doe*. At issue in this case, the US Supreme Court's first case on the topic, were the acceptable limits of disciplining students with disabilities under the (then) Education for All Handicapped Children Act, now the Individuals with Disabilities in Education Act. In its analysis, the court refused to create a dangerousness exception in EHCA, affirming that its "stay-put" provisions prohibit school officials from unilaterally excluding students with disabilities from school for dangerous or disruptive actions that are manifestations of their disabilities while review proceedings are under way. Also, the court affirmed that state officials must provide services directly to students with disabilities when local boards fail to do so.

"John Doe" was an emotionally disturbed student who explosively responded to the taunts of a fellow student by choking the student and then breaking a school window as he was being taken to the principal's office. John was suspended for five days as a result of this behavior. On the fifth day of his suspension, the San Francisco Unified School District Student Placement Committee notified his mother that it was recommending his expulsion and that his suspension would continue indefinitely until the expulsion proceedings were complete.

John, who qualified for special educational services under EHCA, sued the school district and the California Superintendent of Public Instruction, alleging that their disciplinary actions violated the "stay-put" provision of EHCA. Under EHCA "stay-put" provisions, children with disabilities must remain in their existing educational placements pending the completion of any review proceedings unless parents and state or local educational officials agree otherwise. John alleged that the pending expulsion proceedings triggered the "stay-put" provision and that his rights were violated when he was suspended indefinitely.

This case also reached the US Supreme Court, as the issue of John's dangerousness was a contentious one, in light of the desire not to exclude any student from school, per EHCA. The Supreme Court held that the "stay-put" provision of EHCA prohibited state or local school authorities from excluding disabled children from the classroom even for dangerous or disruptive conduct resulting from their disabilities. *Honig* v. *Doe* also is a landmark case as it put to rest the idea of expelling any student from school if the behavior in question is the result of their disability.

5. *Sacramento City Unified Sch. Dist. Bd. of Educ.* v. *Rachel H.* (1990)

This case centered around Rachel H., a young girl with an intellectual disability, and it represents a landmark victory regarding the right of students with disabilities to be educated alongside their nondisabled peers. Rachel's case is considered to be the standard-bearer in helping to determine the least restrictive environment (LRE) in which a student with special needs should be educated.

In this case, Rachel's parents requested that she be placed full-time into a regular classroom for her kindergarten year. The district rejected this request and offered a placement that would divide Rachel's educational time between a special education classroom and a regular education classroom.

This placement would have required Rachel to be moved six times each day between the two classrooms. Her parents appealed this decision and, ultimately, enrolled her in a private school.

Once Rachel enrolled in the private school, she was placed into a regular education classroom, where she performed well and did not require significant amounts of the teacher's attention. Wanting her back in the public school but in the appropriate educational environment, Rachel's parents took the school district to court.

The US Supreme Court affirmed the earlier decision of the Ninth Circuit Court of Appeals, which stated that school officials must consider four factors in making LRE placements: (1) the educational benefits of placing children with disabilities in regular classrooms; (2) the nonacademic benefits of such placements; (3) the effect that the presence of students with disabilities would have on teachers and other children in a class; and (4) the costs of inclusionary placements. Each of these factors must be taken into account when placing students with disabilities in any educational program.

Most LRE decisions are based on school district policies or procedures that directly grew out of the four factors in this decision.

6. *Amanda J. v. Clark County School District* (2001)

Amanda J. was a student in an early childhood education program of the Clark County School District in Las Vegas, Nevada. In March 1995, she was evaluated by a school district psychologist and speech pathologist, both of whom diagnosed Amanda with possible autism. When Amanda's parents asked for copies of her records after the testing, the school district provided them only a summary that did not mention autism.

Without knowledge of the reports indicating possible autism, Amanda's parents participated in two IEP meetings with school officials, and they enrolled her in an early childhood special education program. Later that year, Amanda's family moved to California. Amanda was tested by her California school district, and she was formally diagnosed as a child with autism in January 1996. Her parents asked for a copy of her IEP review, and, for the first time, they saw the reports from Amanda's previous school in Las Vegas, which indicated possible autism. Because her Nevada school failed to accurately follow IDEA procedures, Amanda's parents did not learn of critical medical information concerning their child. This had, in turn, rendered it impossible to provide Amanda with FAPE.

Amanda's parents sued the Clark County School District, and the case made it all the way to the Ninth Circuit Court of Appeals. In their ruling, the appellate court held that, by failing to disclose Amanda's full records in a timely manner, the Clark County School District had denied Amanda FAPE in violation of IDEA. Not only were the parents prevented from participating fully in the design and development of an educational program for their child, the court said that they were denied information concerning their daughter's possible autism, a disease which benefits from early detection and intervention.

This case further defined the right parents have in fully participating in an IEP design. Since many advocates are people with educational and/or special education backgrounds, they often play vital roles in helping to determine what the educational environment for a child with special needs should look like. This is a critical way in which they represent parents, who often do not have the same level of educational and/or special education training.

There are many, many more legal decisions that have helped shape special education policies and practices over the past half century. These six represent different areas of the law, and they help us to define the current environment. They are still some of the most frequently cited and referenced cases when confusion develops among all parties regarding decision-making for students with special needs in both placement and services today.

You can see from these decisions that the type of educational environments described in the first few pages of this book simply will not work in our current environment. These six cases illustrate why. They illustrate for us why schools can no longer teach only those children whose achievement and ability fall within the 30th and 70th percentiles. We must teach all children. And we must ensure that all learners have appropriate and fair access to our curricula. It is not fair: it is equal. Everyone, according to federal law, deserves the right to FAPE.

In the next chapter, we will examine what special education instruction often looks like today. We will demonstrate the types of learning environments and strategies that meet learners' needs, whatever they may be. As we consider the changes in instructional methodology and assessment at the root of special education decisions today, we need to remember that a highly charged legal environment played a major role in getting us to where we are.

 ## Considerations to Ponder

Without diving into the details of each case presented earlier, and without reading the entire decision reached and offered by the courts, you will likely see policies, procedures, and/or behaviors in your own school that clearly have been shaped by these legal decisions. Much of what we do in special education, either from the perspective of the teacher, the student, the parent, or the advocate, has direct ties to these legal decisions and interpretations.

Consider for a few moments how each of the six cases presented above has impacted policies, procedures, and/or behaviors in your school. Then pause and imagine what legal challenges may lie ahead for us. By analyzing areas of IEP writing, conferencing, planning, teaching, assessment, and behavior modification, see if you can identify an area that may not have the appropriate policies, procedures, and/or behaviors created to match what was intended by the re-authorization of IDEA.

Another consideration to ponder is the court cases currently being decided that pertain to special education. It takes many years and appeals for a case to be heard and decided upon by the US Supreme Court. However, you can bet that over the next decade or two, we will experience further refinements in policies and procedures that result directly from high court decisions. Special education is evolving. As it evolves, many different people will need to adapt and learn about new ways of doing things for students. When that happens, we should expect a continuing rise in the number and use of advocates. The more policies and procedures that develop, particularly as a result of legal pressures, the more assurance parents and families will need that their child's school is, in fact, providing the best and most appropriate education possible for their child. Getting this assurance for families will largely be the responsibility of the next generation of advocates. You can be that advocate. Whether you are a parent, a teacher, or a legal advisor, you can help protect the rights of the child you serve. Your time and dedication makes a difference.

If It's Not Legal, Consider It Illegal

Oftentimes in education, we consider things to be illegal only when there is documented legal action or when we know we won't get caught doing them. While that may sound like an unfair condemnation of educators, please know that our intent is merely to point out the somewhat obvious.

When you think about each of the court cases discussed earlier in this chapter, you must recognize that the school or district was violating the intent of IDEA in each and every case. We do not believe that doing so was their intent. They were merely doing what they believed was good for the child and within their power to do. However, until something is verified, codified, or turned into a process or procedure, we typically do what we believe is best, not necessarily what is legally required of us, in most of our schools. There are many students across the country who are not receiving the most appropriate services they should be receiving. This is not because of bad intent, but because of unclear regulation, or bad past practices, or an administrative directive, or a lack of qualified personnel, or, or, or . . . You get the picture.

Similarly, there are many schools that are violating legal requirements, often due to a lack of resources. As we can see from case law, it is expensive to give students with certain disabilities fair and appropriate access to the curriculum. Likewise, it often is challenging to find teachers with the qualifications to provide appropriate instruction to students with certain learning needs. Also, our facilities prevent us from doing some things in the manner that would suit a child's needs best.

In short, providing the access for all students to learn in the least restrictive and most appropriate environment is beyond challenging in some of our schools. As a result, we typically have resorted to characterizing things as being illegal only if somebody calls us out for them. We need to stop thinking that way. While none of us have the resources to ensure that all students, regardless of need, have access to the least restrictive learning environment, we can at least recognize the great efforts we must expend to meet those needs as closely as possible. Just because a school or a teacher is not caught providing a subpar experience to students, it is not excusable to think that all is fine as long as they don't get caught. We like to say that everything which is not legal is illegal. We like to challenge ourselves to fight for all students and to do what the law requires, at a minimum. We do not believe in judging those schools or teachers who do not have the means or abilities to do what is best for all children. Instead, we believe in helping them learn and in assisting them in fighting for resources.

Conclusion

Far from being the definitive legal source for special education challenges and decisions, this chapter provides insight into the legal thoughts that have governed the past half century relative to special education. Legal positions can lean more conservatively or more liberally as Supreme Court justices change, and, for that reason, it always is wise to pay attention to the makeup of the highest court in our land.

We can see that much of what we do with and for students with special needs today has arisen out of legal challenges and decisions. It is wise to conclude that more challenges will arise and more decisions will be reached, which will cause processes for students with special needs to change. Instead of sitting idly by and being reactive, all educators should proactively ensure that they are doing everything possible and appropriate to meet all students' needs. When student needs are the foundation of all teaching and learning decisions, then it is far less likely that a legal decision in the future will cause you to substantially change your practices.

2

The Evolution of Instruction

In this chapter, we emphasize how the understanding and development of instructional practices helped provide students with multiple ways to approach learning. In recognition of the great diversity of all learners, whether identified as needing special services or not, we give examples of how a particular concept can be taught and how learning can be demonstrated in diverse ways. We advise readers that creative ways must be discovered to assist children in accessing the curriculum in the least restrictive, most equal, and appropriate way. Special education practices, procedures, and strategies are useful to all learners.

The momentum gained from the success of landmark legislation passed by the Supreme Court of the United States reviewed in Chapter 1 was a catalyst for change in 21st-century public education instructional practices. The culture of what had been widely accepted pedagogical methods among educators, once perceived as uniform for all, evolved into a much more prescriptive and deliberate approach to cater for the learning styles and instructionally diverse needs of each learner. With the passing of many key pieces of legislation, federal lawmakers were now charged with defining the new parameters of how special education teachers would provide and deliver services to students with disabilities in the regular education classroom. Lawmakers, at first, were not as worried about the practical implications of the legislation, but rather the theoretical implications. It was time for public schools to educate all students;

therefore, students with disabilities needed additional resources. A law was passed, and a mandate was issued. Public schools across the country heard the mandate loud and clear and began implementing the changes based on their own individual interpretation of the law. This led to some confusion, and eventual frustration by lawmakers with how special education services were being implemented across the country.

The theory developed by federal lawmakers behind the legislative term "least restrictive environment" was that the student or students with the identified disability would be educated and receive special education services to the furthest extent possible in the same environment as their typically developing peers. Lawmakers, however, often failed to account for the fact that educating a child in an individualized manner takes significantly more resources, time, and collaboration to plan and implement on the educator's part. Teachers and administrators were left feeling that the special education services the districts were providing needed to match the academic needs of the student with the disability first, then the social needs of the student with the disability second. After more than fifteen years had passed since the original legislation, the great controversy between the federal government and public schools over what the term "least restrictive environment" actually requires escalated to become a huge debate in how special education services would look inside a regular education classroom.

Over the last two decades, public school classrooms looked and felt different, depending on how the public school district interpreted the law of "least restrictive environment". The early years were filled with many types of "pull-out" instructional models. Some included, but were not limited to, 80 percent pull-out models. This meant that the identified student would be "pulled" from his/her regular education setting to be educated in an alternative setting for nearly 80 percent of the classroom day! Lawmakers felt that this was not an accurate interpretation of the law and urged public schools to "push in" special education services to increase the amount of time students spent with their typical peers. This led to the development of terms like "inclusion" and "mainstreaming". Educators and administrators worked hard to ensure students were achieving academic success by constantly "tweaking the curriculum" to adapt it to the special needs learners. This meant that lessons were re-written, tests were modified, and accommodations were made on a continual basis. All of this took a considerable amount of time and resources, which made public school districts frustrated. The amount of dollars public school districts were spending on special education services did not seem to align with the dollars received from the federal government. The districts cried out to lawmakers to alleviate the pressure of "push-in" special education services or there would be a demand for an increase in federal funding. Lawmakers responded with a clear "no". Lawmakers put pressure on educators to conduct lessons which helped students learn in a way that was not only academically motivating and stimulating, but socially motivating and stimulating as well. Research proved that students needed the environmental support of their typically developing peers to remain part of a learning culture that was driven to succeed. So, instead of awarding more funds or alleviating the pressure of a more inclusive educational approach, lawmakers mandated that more efforts be made on the part of public schools to educate every type of student in such a way that all students got what they needed without being taken "away" from their original learning environment. Educators continued to evaluate their instructional practices. Slowly, classrooms evolved to consist of diverse types of learners, learning together. The special education teacher began to come inside the regular education classroom and monitor the special education students, providing assistance only where needed, while the regular education teacher directed the lesson. It wasn't perfect, but at least all of the students were learning together. As a result of this evolution, it turned out that it was also easier for teachers to develop measurable assessments for all learners, aligned with state or national standards, because teachers could now tailor a lesson with a specific standard in mind, instruct the student according to the needs of his/her learning style, and develop an assessment which measured the mastery of that standard. The implications of this instructional culture shift meant that general education teachers were not just teaching students with disabilities using a specific *practice* (designed only for the needs of an exceptional learner), but rather teaching all learners how to use specific *strategies* universally that were prescriptively and deliberatively applied to students of all levels and abilities.

The federal government was more appreciative of the effort public schools were making; however, it didn't completely solve the problem with accommodating the needs of all learners. Regular education teachers began to feel like they were doing all the "work", while the special education teachers stood on the side and "assisted". Districts knew that it wasn't fair for one highly qualified teacher to be standing on the "sidelines" doing less while another highly qualified teacher was doing the major part of the instruction. Researchers began to develop new and improved models of educational teams, which led to the concept of "team-teaching". The look and feel of regular education classrooms changed again. This time, students with different learning needs were still together, but the way they were learning was what changed. Two teachers, with completely different qualifications, were educating two types of students within the same setting at the same time. This was co-teaching. It may look different from situation to situation, but the concept was the same. Now, *both* teachers were responsible for *all* learners, as well as the planning, the teaching, and the assessment of the lesson. Problem solved, right? Well, almost. There was still the question of which student went with which teacher. And then there were the gifted students. Who served those types of learners?

All of this gave rise to the theory of Universal Design for Learning (UDL). The previously coined architectural term "Universal Design for Learning" emerged as a new and inclusive learning theory, complete with instructional implications and principles, which aligned very nicely with the previously established special education initiatives resulting from legislative decisions for students with disabilities. Originally just an architectural term, used to implement the defining principles of the Americans with Disabilities Act related only to providing equal access to public facilities for all people way back in early 1990, UDL became the harbinger of change for educators to implement principles related to instructional design in an inclusive setting.

Foundational Perspective of Universal Design for Learning

Originally coined by architect Ron Mace, Universal Design for Learning was established as a result of the Americans with Disabilities Act of 1990. The theory behind this concept was, as stated above, simply architectural in nature. It was used as part of the design process to create universal access to public buildings regardless of one's physical ability. Over time, this concept evolved into a theoretical approach for educational researchers. It paved the way for the development of a set of three principles, guiding teachers today to deliver instruction and provide access to materials used for all learners. Simply put, the goal of UDL now is to remove limits – physical, emotional, social, cognitive, and technological – to learning. It is a truly collaborative, inclusive, and universal model for educators in 21st-century classrooms.

Harvard's Graduate School of Education faculty member David Rose, a leading researcher and lecturer in education today, saw the need for the curriculum to adapt to the learner. He theorized that it wasn't the students, but the curriculum that was disabled. He worked together with neuropsychologists at North Shore Children's Hospital in Boston to create a system of evaluating poor-performing students. This led to the creation of the Center for Applied Special Technology (CAST). Rose (2014) states:

> UDL is not going to look exactly the same for every kid or every classroom. We don't want to "boxify" the whole approach or make teachers follow a script. We want teachers who are carefully watching their students and using their informed discretion about what's working and what's not.

Figure 2.1 The Three Guiding Principles for Universal Design for Learning

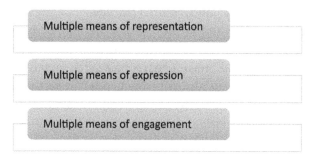

Rose and his team of researchers and educators have adopted the principles for UDL shown in Figure 2.1.

Defining the Three Principles

1. Multiple Means of Representation – to Give Learners Various Ways to
Acquire Knowledge
The teacher will provide a variety of means and modes to present concepts to a student in the manner that is most suited to the needs of student's individual learning in order to provide the student with the ability to acquire the content and master the skill.

Example
Susan, an average fourth grader, was struggling with her double-digit multiplication algorithms. She used the textbook, and the instructions the teacher had given her, to follow the step-by-step process of multiplying 24 × 42. Every time she got to the third step of the multiplication process, she ended up with the incorrect digits. It seemed like there were too many steps to follow, and Susan got confused. As a result, she failed her quiz. Susan's teacher asked her why she was confused about how to solve the problem when she had been given specific, step-by-step instructions using the textbook the previous day. Susan told her, "There are too many steps! If I mess up one of the digits in the third step of the problem, it makes my whole answer wrong."

Later that evening, the teacher began to reflect on Susan and her problem. Even though Susan usually got As or Bs on all of her math assignments, this particular algorithm was just not conducive to Susan's understanding of the concept. It wasn't fair that Susan was failing her quiz because there were too many steps to the problem. It also wasn't fair to Susan that the textbook the teacher was using only explained multiplication in one specific way. Susan's teacher reviewed the national standard that aligned with the lesson. It stated: "Multiply two two-digit numbers, using strategies based on place value and the properties of operations. Illustrate and explain the calculation by using equations, rectangular arrays and/or area models."

Susan's teacher realized that although the algorithm in the textbook met the requirement of the state standard, it did not allow Susan to access the curriculum in a way that met Susan's learning needs. Susan's inability to neurologically process this type of algorithm was not due to the fact that she had a suspected disability, but due to the fact that she was more of a visual learner (a learner who creates concepts using images) rather than a written learner. She may not have been ready to developmentally handle the more abstract process of this type of textbook algorithm. Therefore, it was in Susan's best interest that her teacher utilize the first principle of the UDL – "multiple means of representation" – to help Susan access the curriculum in a manner that was suited to her individual learning needs.

The following day, Susan's teacher wrote the same problem at the top of Susan's paper. Susan slumped down in her chair with frustration. "Not this *again*!", she said.

The teacher said, "Think of this problem like a set of groups or pictures. If you have 20 boxes of 40 pencils, how many do you have?"

Susan replied, "That's easy . . . 800!"

The teacher said, "Then if you had 40 boxes with 4 pencils in each, how many do you have?"

Susan said, "160!"

The teacher continued by guiding her through the same process for the remainder of the problem. The algorithm the teacher used to represent the multiplication model helped Susan to visualize the numbers in groups and pictures rather than just in step-by-step numerical form. It also made it much easier to visualize the groups represented by calling them pencils in boxes. Susan's teacher gave her a quiz later in the day on two-digit multiplication numbers. She allowed Susan to use the new algorithm she had taught her. Susan's teacher had now used an alternative algorithm called "partial products method". Clearly, this differentiated method of representing the curriculum led to the success of Susan understanding the concept and developing mastery. It also incorporated the second principle of UDL, providing Susan a chance to demonstrate her understanding using an alternative method of expression, as discussed below.

2. Multiple Means of Expression – to Give Learners Alternative Ways to Demonstrate Knowledge
The teacher will offer the student multiple ways to demonstrate mastery of the content. The student will have a choice of demonstrating acquired knowledge through modalities that include, but are not limited to, written, verbal, kinesthetic, and visual demonstrations.

Example

Levon, a bright and high-achieving sixth grader, was given a writing assignment that aligned with the sixth grade Common Core standard of writing a narrative related to a real or imagined experience. The writing assignment was complex, requiring Levon to utilize transitional words, phrases, relative descriptive details, events, characters, and a strong conclusion. Even for Levon, this was a daunting task. Typically, Levon was able to outperform his peers on most assignments, as he worked quickly and completed his work with accuracy. Writing, however, required stamina, which was not one of his strengths. Levon's teacher was aware that Levon might devote less effort to this particular task because of the tremendous amount of concentration it would take to complete it. The teacher made the decision to offer Levon a different modality of demonstrating this content knowledge in order to motivate Levon to complete the assignment to the best of his ability. Levon was very verbal, often articulating words and phrases using vocabulary which was well above his grade level. He spoke both naturally and intelligently in front of peers. The teacher knew that Levon would have to write his narrative as part of the assignment, but before he wrote it, he could use technology to verbally create it and record it. That way, it would seem as though it wasn't that daunting an assignment. Levon took the recording device to a quiet space in the school and began to create a narrative based on a real-life experience. After three recordings, he felt sure he had completed his assignment with accuracy. When he played the recording for the teacher, he was graded using the same rubric that had been used for the rest of the class. Levon received an A. Later, when Levon had small amounts of spare time, the teacher asked him to transcribe his verbal work into a written work in order to complete the assignment as a written task. After that, Levon felt much better about his ability to write by being given a chance to demonstrate his knowledge verbally first. Levon spent the remainder of the year completing all of his writing assignments in this manner. Not only did he achieve a high success rate of completing written assignments verbally first, but he was also intrinsically motivated to do the work based on the fact that he enjoyed the opportunity to speak. He was engaged and able to express his knowledge accurately. The idea that Levon's teacher used an alternative method of expression and an intrinsically motivating method of engagement (as discussed below) helped Levon build self-confidence in his ability to write well.

3. Multiple Means of Engagement – Using Learner Interests, Creating Appropriate Challenges, and Motivating Students Intrinsically to Help Achieve Content Mastery

Example

Mrs. Smith's third grade class was completing a thematic unit on "Earth in the Universe". The students were excited about the project, because it involved creating models of the solar system. However, Mrs. Smith knew that this project would not be easy for all of her students, because it had been designed for small groups to create and build the solar system together. She knew that conflicts would arise between those students who loved the idea of "being in charge". Mrs. Smith decided to brainstorm ways to motivate all of her students to work on the project both as teams in groups and individually using their strengths. She created four groups. Each of the four groups had five members. The groups would all be graded using the same rubric, but the jobs of each of the five members would vary according to the students' interests, abilities, and social skills. The students would be evaluated on both their individual responsibilities and their group responsibilities. The scores would then be combined to form a final score for each member of the group. She began developing her groups by determining the strengths of the first group of students she chose. Group A consisted of five students: John, Mary, Chris, Steve, and Mickey. Mickey was talented at writing, and he loved summarizing stories. Mary was an outstanding artist. Chris loved to talk. John was a stickler for details, and he generated detailed lists for everything he did. Steve was great at researching. Mrs. Smith decided that each group member would be assigned specific tasks within the group. The tasks would look like those in Figure 2.2.

Mrs. Smith did this for all four of her groups, ensuring that each student was given tasks that were intrinsically motivating, yet challenging, in order to

Figure 2.2 Tasks Assigned to Each Student

Mary
Draw or develop a visual model of the universe (using all the appropriate terms and details needed to define Earth's location relative to the Sun and Moon). Discuss with the group for feedback.

John
Create a detailed list of all the items needed on Mary's model, ensuring Mary has an accurate representation. Give the list to Mary for feedback.

Steve
Research and develop ideas about about how the model could be created (poster, 3-D design, trifold, etc.). Share the ideas with Mary and John.

Mickey
Create a written summary of the final project using the research Steve and John have submitted.

Chris
Work with Mickey to discuss how the written work will be presented in front of the class. Present the written work to the class.

engage the students to work to their fullest potential. In the end, as Mrs. Smith reflected on the project, she saw that it was successful. With only a few small conflicts, Mrs. Smith decided this was the way she would organize all future group projects. What Mrs. Smith learned was that the students not only achieved academic success, but also the emotional feelings of well-being from the project, by using the principles created by Rose and his team of researchers.

Conclusion

Current research on best practices in education shows increasing evidence that all students, regardless of ability, are demonstrating that they learn best with a more individualized, deliberate, and meaningful instructional approach. As both educators and parents, we believe it is important to motivate students both at school and at home to complete tasks in such a way that inspires them to use their strengths, while acknowledging and working on their weaknesses. A student may or may not have an identified disability to utilize the principles of UDL. The most important thing to remember is that the principles are applied according to the needs of the whole student, not just according to the type of disability.

 ## Considerations to Ponder

How can parents partner with teachers to incorporate UDL principles both at home and at school?

Glad you asked! Teachers and parents can easily utilize the principles of UDL. That is the reason the principles are defined as "universal": they apply to everyone, everywhere, regardless of age, race, religion, ability, or social status. We can all benefit from understanding and applying these principles in a variety of ways during everyday activities. Listed below are some simple suggestions on how to build UDL into your home/school partnership. Use the worksheet at the end of this chapter to make notes on all the ways UDL has been easily incorporated into school and home activities.

Tips and Tricks for a Collaborative UDL Partnership at Home and at School
- ◆ Explore websites related to UDL: www.udlcenter.org and www.cast.org.
- ◆ Offer the student a variety of ways to complete homework assignments utilizing different modalities for engagement and expression (computers, voice recorders, voice-to-text devices, posters, movement, verbal expression, etc.).

◆ Give active students opportunities to use their kinesthetic abilities to complete tasks or to take short breaks from assignments which require stamina and complicated executive functioning skills that involve planning, working memory, self-monitoring, impulse control, task initiation, organization, flexible thinking, and emotional control. See www.understood.org.

◆ Develop places in the home and at school that are conducive to studying and learning (for example, make a "homework tent" – complete with snacks, a portable light, a comfy pillow, and a timer). Sometimes the motivation to initiate a task comes from knowing that the environment feels "safe" and "exclusive" to the learner. It becomes a special place, made just for the student, like an office would be for an adult.

◆ Create a shared checklist of extrinsic motivators to use both at home and at school that will help the student maintain a strong desire to initiate tasks independently. The list should include things the student enjoys receiving as a reward, such as video game time, television time, a cookie or snack, a sticker, or time with a friend. As time passes, generate a new list of extrinsic motivators to keep the student's level of interest high.

◆ Provide choices in the amount of time needed for task completion. This will give the student an opportunity to have control over when he/she will complete the assignment. The student may realize that he/she has to do the homework, but the homework may not all have to be completed in one sitting. It can be broken up over several fifteen-minute blocks of time, depending on the student's level of energy and focus at the time.

◆ Give the student an opportunity to do the assignment on a different topic that is of more interest to him/her. For example, if the writing assignment is based on completing a narrative, why not give the student a choice of what kind of narrative to write instead of insisting that the student write an already pre-determined topic. After all, the evaluation of the learning outcome should be based on how well the student completed the narrative, not on what type of narrative the student chose.

◆ Teachers can collaborate with other teachers (and parents) to plan activities that involve high levels of content integration and engagement (for example, problem-based learning, service learning, etc.), so that students learn content developed around a theme.

Provide students with the opportunity to evaluate assignments after completion. Ask probing questions, such as: *Did you enjoy this task? Why or why not? What would have made it more interesting? What did you like about this task? What was the most challenging part of this task?*

The Reflection Activity Worksheet on the following pages is a reproducible resource for both teachers and parents to use at home or at school. The concept of UDL is not new, but is truly an important part of how education has evolved into a collaborative yet highly individualized and deliberate structure. As more research is conducted, psychologists and neurologists will learn even more about how to understand and develop the human brain. In the end, we are all learning that our differences make us even more alike.

Reflection Activity Worksheet

1. What principle of UDL have you already been implementing at home or at school? What was the task, and how did you apply the principle?

_____

_____

_____

_____

_____

_____

2. What principle of UDL did you learn more about?

_____

_____

_____

_____

_____

_____

3. List two examples of ways to use the UDL principle of *Multiple Means of Expression* at home or at school.

_____

_____

_____

_____

_____

_____

4. Choose one task to implement all three principles of UDL for a student. This task should be completed both at home and at school in partnership with the parent(s).

_____

_____

5. Evaluate the task by including the teacher, the parent(s), and the student? Discuss and write in the section below what worked and what didn't work. Save the evaluation in a student folder to use as a resource on how best to apply the principles of UDL for this student in future tasks.

_____

_____

_____

_____

_____

_____

_____

_____

_____

_____

_____

_____

_____

3

The Individualized Education Plan (IEP) Process

The process for generating, implementing, and evaluating the Individualized Education Plan has the same components no matter where your school is located. It's important to truly understand the process and the purpose for each step in the process. Parents and advocates really can help improve the process, and their input can lead to a better IEP. In this chapter, Julie Fiore reflects on her own educational experiences and how they have impacted her perception of learning and influenced the way she has developed her instructional methods.

It is not by accident that parents and public educators participate together in the Individualized Education Plan (IEP) process today. As you already have read in Chapter 1, there were many hard-won legislative battles during the last several decades which helped to establish the rights of students with suspected disabilities to be evaluated and educated appropriately with their typically developing peers. As you begin to read this chapter, keep in mind that what you may have experienced as a student in public education has dramatically changed today, and not just for the good of students with disabilities, but for all learners. Picture yourself as you read through the historical aspects of public education. Then imagine yourself as a student today. *How can you compare 21st-century learning with the learning you experienced during your childhood years?* Our hope is that as you read this chapter, the most important information you glean is that we are all truly individuals, with individual needs, goals, and plans. The heart of education is that it is universally important for everyone, no matter what you want to achieve in life.

Historically, teachers educated students in classrooms where learners were more alike than they were different. During the 1960s, 1970s, and 1980s, instruction was developed and implemented according to grade level, age, and ability. Other considerations included arranging students according to sex or particular interest, but more often than not, ability grouping remained the most popular way to teach, because the planning was not done by several people, but by one person: the classroom teacher. The result of these homogeneous (like) groupings meant that the planning and focus of student learning was aligned with what the teacher wanted all students to learn rather than with what the individual learner needed in order to be successful. As you think back to your experiences of elementary school, do you remember being taught in a large group, with the teacher writing on the chalkboard in the front of the room? Our guess is that you were part of a homogeneous group, learning the same material in the same way the rest of the group learned. You probably also remember that most of the students in your group were working in or around your same level.

I can remember when I was in fifth grade, and at the beginning of the year the teacher gave us all assessments, determined our levels, and created a "group" that we would remain in for the entire year. For reading, I was in the "high" group, and for math, I was in the "low" group. It didn't take me long to figure out that I must be "bad" at math and "good" at reading. This created a sense of belief in myself that my abilities couldn't be changed. I was just going to be "bad" at math for the rest of my life and "good" at reading for the rest of my life. It wasn't until I was in college, studying to be a teacher myself, that a professor told me I was an excellent math student. He stated, and I quote: "Why are you getting additional help in math? You clearly know everything you need to know about the formulas. You just lack confidence!" I sat back, with my arms folded across my chest, staring at this man. I then had an epiphany, and I was so angry and relieved at the very same time. I realized that the teachers who had taught me simply did what was easiest for them, and not what was best for me. I had been conditioned to believe that I was in a "group" of learners that was either "high" or "low", and that belief about myself had never been altered.

I then began to reflect on my entire educational background. I remember that "outliers", or the students with varied learning needs, were often forced to mold to the majority. Teaching, for the most part, was very "whole-group", with little room for individualized instruction, so the students with some learning differences were just placed in ability groups, and no additional services were provided. This practice of educating students as a whole group often prevented the students with some type of exceptionality from developing to reach their potential. I may or may not have had a disability in math, but it didn't matter. *What did matter was that the teacher never accommodated my learning needs.* She simply plopped me in a group and taught me the same material at a slower pace. Now, luckily, I managed to adapt to that style of teaching just like many students did in that era. We didn't have any other choice. Only students who were extremely gifted or severely disabled were given services outside of the classroom to accommodate their needs. So I must have developed coping strategies, because in later years, I did manage to be successful in math.

The Exceptional Learner

Fast-forward to public education today, and you will see how teaching and learning have evolved to meet the needs of the individual learner. As discussed in Chapter 1, a number of important legislative decisions were implemented over the last several decades which not only established a process for identifying a student with exceptional needs, but required funding on both federal and state levels to provide resources needed to educate the student. The goal of these laws was not only to protect the right of students with disabilities, but also to ensure students with disabilities received the same access to a free appropriate public education (FAPE) as their typically developing peers. This set a historical precedent for the development of individualized learning and began the course for what is now called "differentiated instruction", not only because it benefitted students with disabilities, but because it taught educators that we all learn differently, and teaching should adapt to the learner, regardless of the students' ability.

Today, the historical precedent (set for students with disabilities) paved the way for a universal teaching and learning approach, which helped to "equalize" instruction for all types of learners. When I said "equalize", I meant that all students, regardless of their levels or abilities, were learning at their appropriate developmental level, using the same content, but with varied types of pedagogical methods designed to ensure that learning is acquired and internalized specifically for each learner.

This is called *differentiation*. The term "differentiation", coined by Dr. Virgil Ward (1961), offered a more "prescriptive" approach to instructional design to meet the needs of various types of students within the same classroom. As you read on, you will see how the implementation of special education laws affected general education and helped to establish practices which were universally beneficial for all learners.

The Instructional Team: Changing "Me" to "We"

Teachers in the 21st-century classroom are working harder than ever to measure student growth, plan prescriptive lessons, and collaborate with other colleagues to promote success, both inside and outside the classroom. Teachers are also increasingly relying on parent support and input in order to understand how best to serve the students. This is not only required by law, but according to research, is best practice. This type of collaborative instruction establishes a "team" or community of support for the student. As you can see, this means that teaching really has evolved from being a very isolated and lonely profession to a very interdependent and cooperative one.

The "team", as it is called – special education teacher, regular education teacher, school psychologist, parent(s), administration, and paraprofessionals – uses all kinds of the information, collected from small and large pieces of data, like test scores, checklists, and anecdotal information, relevant to the child, to develop an IEP. The IEP is a legally binding document which encompasses a tremendous amount of evidence, gathered over time, to prove that additional resources and services are needed to meet the needs of the learner, who is deemed "exceptional" or outside the norm of a typical learner.

You might now be wondering how evidence is gathered to prove that a student qualifies for special education services and an IEP. First of all, the evidence must be collected by the team over a long period, analyzed, and reported out in order to prove that the student being evaluated is learning significantly above or below that of his/her typically developing peers. Gathering data or evidence is not just the teacher's job. It is the job of every person on the team. After all, the evolution of teaching has moved from "teacher-centered learning" to "student-centered learning", which means that the focus is on the student, not the teacher. So the data must show that the student has a need, across a wide variety of settings, significant enough to warrant the development of an IEP and the services and funding that the IEP requires. The special education process is a long one, but definitely worthwhile if it means that the student will be successful as a result (Figure 3.1).

This means it gives the exceptional learner the right to have specifically designed, measurable goals and resources according to the requirements of state and federal law. These specifically designed, measurable goals and resources allow exceptional learners to access the curriculum in a way that is fair for their ability, so that they, too, may participate in learning as closely as possible to their typically developing peers who do not have a disability.

Figure 3.1 Process of Special Education

Note: This chart is an example of how services are designed to match the needs of the child. As the child grows and develops, the IEP grows and develops along with the child.

Gathering Evidence: Who, What, When, and Where

You may remember a few students during your elementary years who left the classroom with an additional teacher or some type of therapist to receive "additional help". Or perhaps you were the one receiving additional help. Think back to how it must have felt to be "pulled" from the group to receive that extra help. I remember watching the students who received additional services leave the room. I had mixed feelings. Part of me felt sorry for them, while part of me envied them. *Where were they going? What would they be doing? Who worked with them, and why?*

Specialized instruction today is most often provided in the same classroom with the rest of the students. Why, you might ask? The Individuals with Disabilities Education Act (IDEA) requires that students be educated in their least restrictive environment (LRE) as much as possible in order to meet their individual educational needs. This means that the law states that taking students out of the natural learning environment with their typically developing peers to learn is not only detrimental to their social development, but to their cognitive development as well. As I begin to describe the logistics of the IEP process, think about the role of the "team", then think about the student. *If you were the student being "pulled" to receive additional instruction many years ago, how would you want your IEP to be today? What would be different?*

The IEP process may not always be initiated by the teacher. Sometimes a parent or a medical professional requests a formal evaluation based on observations and data collected which point to a suspected disability. If the teacher suspects a disability, many states require that preliminary interventions be used first to rule out any other underlying causes of the child's lack of success in school before a formal evaluation can occur. This process is called *Response to Intervention (RtI)*. RtI is usually implemented for a specific period, across a wide variety of settings, and can include, but is not limited to, academic interventions, behavioral interventions, and social interventions. It is designed to help the child by providing research-based strategies implemented within the child's typical peer group, on a short-term basis, to correct a deficiency in academic, social, or emotional growth without the work of a formal evaluation process and special education services. Oftentimes, RtI is all that is needed to get a student "back on track", which saves the district thousands of dollars in wasted special education funds and prevents students from being "labeled" with a disability.

If the data shows that research-based interventions or RtI did not help the student, then the teacher, parent, or medical provider may request that the student be formally evaluated for special education services. Thus, the school psychologist is contacted by the team and the team submits a written request for a formal evaluation. If you are a teacher in a public school setting, you may be familiar with this process. What you may not know is that your contribution to the formal evaluation process is incredibly powerful and can have a lasting effect on the planning and implementation of a child's IEP. Most teachers and parents today are extremely busy. However, knowing what information to submit to the school psychologist for the formal evaluation is vital. Depending on the district and its requirements, you may be asked to fill out a variety of assessments. These assessments are important because they reflect your objective viewpoint on the child's progress. You should be able to use the data you have collected, your team has collected, and any anecdotal information, to help you complete the assessments. Whether you are a parent or a teacher, to make the instrument a valid and reliable one, you should not use subjective information. For example, an objective anecdotal statement regarding Johnny's behavior may look like this: *"Johnny refuses to participate in math during three out of four lessons per week. During this time, Johnny is observed sitting at his desk, drawing on a piece of paper."* This type of information simply states an observed behavior. You cannot tell from this information whether Johnny is being bad or good. He is just not participating. It is up to the evaluating team to determine why Johnny is not participating. Your job as an assessor is only to show that Johnny is not on task. All of the information gathered by the team may reveal why Johnny is not participating. *Let the data speak.*

In contrast to the example above, a subjective anecdotal statement regarding Johnny's behavior may look like this: *"Johnny is rude and defiant. He never listens in math, and because of that, he is failing."* This doesn't tell the psychologist what he is doing. *How do you know Johnny is being rude and defiant? What evidence proves that?* Your job is to look at what you see and hear. You saw that Johnny wasn't participating, was doodling in his notebook, and you did not hear him speak or participate in class. He isn't necessarily being rude, so that assumption may be unfair. Write down facts, and don't make assumptions. Johnny may be overwhelmed with the academic content, and his drawing may be a way to escape or to cope. The heart of writing a good IEP is that it is data-driven and it is team-based. All personal feelings about Johnny, his issues, and any other opinions must be pushed aside for the development of an accurate IEP. Remember, the goal is not to judge Johnny, but to help Johnny be successful. Your contribution as a parent or a teacher will undoubtedly affect the outcome of his initial IEP. Plan with the end in mind. *What do you want Johnny to be able to do? Do you want to see him happily participating in a math lesson? Do you want him having fun while he engages in learning with his typical peers?* Picture Johnny being successful, remove judgments, stereotypes, and biases, and be part of the solution. Focusing on the problem only perpetuates it. Focusing on the solution encourages everyone else in the team to do the same.

Discussing the Data: Who and What

Remember, the development of the IEP is a team process. The data from the team, not just from the parent or the teacher, shapes how the IEP is developed. This is why it is important to have many observers collecting data. In most cases, the "who" in a team consists of a regular education teacher, a paraprofessional working with the student, a parent, a medical provider, a psychologist, and if needed, another teacher, such as an art or music teacher. The purpose of knowing who is contributing is twofold: your evidence may be consistent with other evidence, which helps prove that the same observations are being made across subject matter and settings, and your evidence may be inconsistent with other evidence, which helps prove that the student may not show the same observable behavior across different subject matter and settings. The power of a team reporting data separately and accurately is that it creates reliable and valid statistics, which helps support or negate the need for an IEP.

The "what" is the data. It is the actual evidence you collect, record, and bring to meetings to report out. If you don't have a tool to collect data, a great little chart you can make yourself is shown in Table 3.1. You can use notebook paper, or you can create it on a computer.

While the chart is simple, it does provide evidence that Johnny was not on task. You can be as descriptive or as simple as you choose. You can observe

Table 3.1 Behavioral Observation Chart

Observable Behavior	Place	Date	Time
Example 1: Johnny was drawing on his paper. He drew a picture of a dinosaur. He asked me a question about dinosaurs, and then he did not speak during the rest of our time working together.	Regular education classroom – Math Lesson	4-15-2017	11:32 a.m.–11:57 a.m.

the behavior for as short or as long as you like, but the most important thing is that you are consistent in your observations. You need to record Johnny's behavior repeatedly during the same time period each day over several weeks to show accurate evidence.

Reviewing the Environment: Where and When

If you are the regular education teacher or parent, you need to complete your assessment(s) in the environment where you work with the child most often. It isn't accurate or appropriate to chase the student while he/she is running down the hallway to recess just to collect data. I can say with certainty, however, that I have seen it done. When one of the team members collects data outside the environmental setting where he/she typically works with the student, it becomes invalid, because that part of the assessment must relate to the setting in which you interact with the student on a daily basis. This is an environmental factor. Now, if you happen to be the paraprofessional who is working with the student at recess, and your job is to collect data at that time, that is fine. Just know that you need to collect data in the setting where and when you most often interact with the student, to demonstrate consistency.

Analyzing the Problem: Why and How

You may remember that earlier (p. 32) I wrote: "Let the data speak." As the team sits down to analyze the data collected over an extended period of time, such as a nine- to eighteen-week period, a pattern may begin to emerge that is both observable and significant for a student's academic history compared to typically developing peers. The team can then disseminate the information to determine what types of environments, stimuli, or antecedents provoke a particular behavior or interaction that causes a student to become off task.

Once the information is analyzed, the team makes determinations about the student's needs in order to begin to develop the IEP. While the team is working to analyze the data, the questions that are helping to drive the decision-making process should be: *Why is this student having trouble reading? How can the team meet the needs of the student and improve his/her ability to read?*

Now, let's look at a hypothetical situation involving a student with low reading scores. Susan, a fourth grader, is achieving poor grades in all subjects except math. She has been observed by her regular education teacher, her reading teacher, and her science teacher over the first ten weeks of school. The data shows that whenever Susan works on grade-level reading material, she is unable to decode at least 50 percent of the words in each sentence. As a result of this, she is also unable to comprehend what she reads, which results in failing test scores on assignments. Susan works very well with her peers when she is completing "hands-on" activities during science. However, when she is asked to read or write during science and reading lessons, she often refuses, or writes information which is not completely relevant to the topic and/or is poorly constructed. Her peers notice that she is unable to understand the content when she reads it independently, so they sometimes read it to her and write for her when they are working in small groups. Susan tells them what to write, and when she does, she gets excellent grades.

The data from the parents' observations over ten weeks shows that Susan is cooperative at home, respects each member of her family, but often struggles to complete her homework assignments, unless they are math assignments. Susan's parents feel that she is too old to be getting much help on her homework and want her to be able to get it done independently. However, Susan is frustrated that she cannot understand what she is reading, so she rarely turns in completed homework assignments in all of her classes except math.

As you review the information, you may notice that this student's case is fairly straightforward. Susan has difficulty with reading and writing in large groups, and benefits from small group interactions where her reading and writing are supported within her typical peer groups. Susan also enjoys "hands-on" activities. The beginning of the IEP is a chance for the team to review what strengths and challenges a student may have, to build on those strengths and challenges, and to begin the process of creating measurable goals, accommodations, and other services the student may need to access the curriculum.

In the next section of this chapter, you will learn about the eight components of an IEP. It is important to note that each section of the IEP is of equal significance. The components are listed in the order in which they are written in a standard IEP. Some states may vary the structure of the IEP, or the IEP may have sections with differing titles. The overall plan, however, is generalized and must be followed according to federal guidelines. As you read each section, you will notice that the hypothetical case study regarding Susan, the fourth grader, has been interwoven into the IEP.

The Eight Components of an IEP

The IEP is comprised of eight important sections (Figure 3.2). Each section is designed to identify and highlight different aspects of this individualized plan for all members of the team in order to provide clear, concise information on how the team will wrap educational services around the needs of the student. The plan is strategically organized to disseminate all of the evidence gathered by the team (who, what, when, where, and why) and to determine the educational plan going forward resulting from this evidence. *It is both a*

Figure 3.2 The Eight Components of an IEP

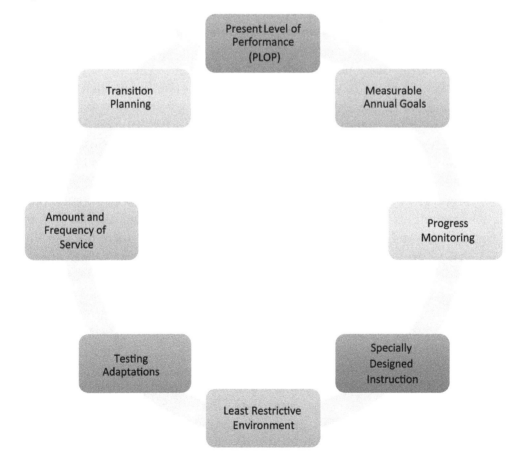

compass for learning and a legally binding contract between the parent and the school. While the IEP provides legal documentation of special education services, it also provides a visual framework for illustrating the collaborative teamwork necessary for education today. It serves to further the cause of cooperative teaching and joint responsibility for student success in 21st-century learning.

Section 1: Present Level of Performance

The first section of the IEP is called Present Level of Performance (PLOP). The PLOP summarizes the current skill profile of the student. It is a "big picture overview" of what the team has observed while working with this student, and establishes the foundational pieces for the remaining components of the IEP. The data from formal assessments as well as some informal observations by the team are used to develop this component of the IEP. The special education teacher typically drafts an IEP prior to the actual meeting in order to provide the context for the final product. However, the team members work together to revise the draft to ensure that all of the important instructional pieces and supports are in place for the student as it is being finalized.

Section 2: Measurable Annual Goals

The next part of the IEP is the Measurable Annual Goals. These goals represent specific, measurable, and achievable objectives of the curriculum, aligned with the Common Core Standards, through which the student will be monitored for progress throughout the IEP year. The goals, while developed by the team of teachers and administrators, must be supported and approved by the parents, and also by the student. The student may have as many goals and objectives as the team determines he/she needs in order to be successful academically and to show growth. It is up to the team to agree on the type and number of goals and objectives placed in the IEP. Typically, the special education teacher will draft sample goals and objectives. Then the team will make a final determination on which goals and objectives are most relevant to the student's deficits in academic or behavioral growth.

In Susan's case, for example, her parent(s) may want Susan to develop more fluency in her reading. Susan's teachers, however, may also want to see Susan develop greater comprehension skills. Those goals are not unreasonable, nor are they exclusive of one another. The teacher and the parent can decide that both goals are worthy of implementing, because they are complementary. This is true teamwork.

Section 3: Progress Monitoring

After the goals are developed and agreed upon, the team then decides how the progress of these goals will be tracked. There are a variety of ways to assess and track goals. Most often the teacher(s) will use a combination of both formal and informal assessments to monitor progress. The progress will then be reported out to the team at the end of grading periods. The parents can also request to meet with any or all of the members of the team to review the progress of their child at any time. Great teachers know that building communication into a daily or weekly phone call or email will go a long way toward preventing misunderstandings and promoting student success. Parents and teachers who collaborate early and often provide a seamless continuum of support, which enables the student to be held accountable for their learning both at school and at home and allows for progress monitoring to be integrated holistically into a student's daily life.

Some examples of various types of progress monitoring include, but are not limited to, checklists, anecdotal observations, criterion-referenced assessments, and norm-referenced assessments. The team decides which type of progress monitoring tools to use, then adds those components to this section of the IEP. The teachers are then responsible for assessing students exactly as the IEP states and providing evidence of those assessments when necessary for the team to analyze and evaluate progress. The key to quality progress monitoring is being consistent and transparent with the data.

Section 4: Specially Designed Instruction

The next section of the IEP details how the team will provide Specially Designed Instruction for the student. Using Susan's case, we can see that Susan benefits by working with her typical peers in small groups within the regular education setting. She also enjoys completing "hands-on activities" and having a variety of modalities in which to read and write. The specially designed instruction will be developed based on this information, because the goal is to utilize Susan's strengths to help intrinsically motivate her to succeed.

Susan's team will decide on the most appropriate research-based interventions, how often she will receive the interventions, and where the interventions will be implemented. Some examples of these interventions may include, but are not limited to, listening to books on tape, paired reading, repeated reading, main-idea mapping, using graphic organizers, and much more. This specially designed instruction utilizes Susan's strengths while implementing research-based interventions to help Susan meet the measurable goals and objectives from Section 2 of the IEP. This creates a scientifically proven plan that interests and motivates Susan to learn, which fosters success and achievement of her goals and objectives.

Section 5: Least Restrictive Environment

After the Specially Designed Instruction section of the IEP is developed, the team will then decide on the location of service. The PLOP data from the first section of the IEP proved Susan was most successful when working in the regular education classroom setting with her typically developing peers. The team needs to ensure that this section of the IEP is not only beneficial to the student, but also aligns with the law by offering special education services in the student's LRE. *The LRE is the environment that allows the student to be educated as much as possible with his/her typically developing peers.* In Susan's case, it was easy to determine that the services she was going to receive needed to be in the regular education classroom setting, because the data proved that she was more successful there than in a more restrictive environment, such as a resource room. So the final determination of the team will likely be that she will be most successful and legally compliant when she receives the specially designed services in the regular education setting.

Section 6: Testing Adaptations

Once the student's LRE has been determined by the team, Testing Adaptations can be established for the student. School districts are responsible for using a variety of tests to monitor progress and track achievement rates for grade levels and graduation. Students who have IEPs must be given appropriate adaptations when necessary in order to give them a fair chance of achieving a score that is within the range of their typically developing peers.

Typical testing adaptations or accommodations used for IEP students include, but are not limited to, extended time, small group testing, noise-canceling headphones, reader, scribe, frequent breaks, and enlarged print. The team will review the IEP to determine which accommodations are suitable for each student, depending on his/her disability, and then align those accommodations with what is allowable according to state guidelines. Students who struggle with reading are not typically allowed to have a reader for the text on which they are being assessed. They are, however, allowed to have a reader for the question-and-answer choices at the end of each text section.

Susan's testing accommodations could be having extended time, working in a small group, having questions and answers read aloud, and frequent breaks. The team will not only need to provide those accommodations during state-mandated testing, but over the entire school year during any formal assessments, in order to demonstrate consistency in providing testing accommodations. Susan and/or her parents may request that the testing accommodations be changed as the year progresses if Susan does not feel she needs the additional support in order to be successful. If this occurs, the IEP team will need to reconvene with Susan and attach an amendment to the original IEP that states which testing accommodations have been changed and the dates when the changes will take effect.

Section 7: Amount and Frequency of Service

When you read about Specially Designed Instruction in Section 4, you may have wondered where and how often the services will be provided for the student. Each student is different. The team will determine the most appropriate place for the specially designed instruction to take place and the frequency with which it will be administered. The team will also make decisions about who will provide the service. In most cases, the service must be provided by the special education teacher, but if the setting for the specially designed instruction is a regular education classroom, the regular education teacher may share the responsibility for administering specially designed instruction cooperatively with the special education teacher.

In Susan's case, her LRE was determined to be the regular education classroom, so both the special education teacher and the regular education teacher would be responsible for providing specially designed services. In Susan's case, it would be typical for her to receive specially designed instruction about 40 minutes per day, five days per week. As Susan's progress is monitored, that amount of time can be adjusted if the team feels it is not enough to support her in reading. Again, the need for a change in service would require the team to reconvene and create an amendment to the original IEP, which would then need to be signed off by the parents.

Section 8: Transition Planning

The final section of the IEP contains the information the team needs to determine how the student will move from the support of the public school system to an independent lifestyle upon graduation. IEPs established in the public school system are in place from ages 3 to 21. When a student graduates, the transition plan created in Section 8 outlines and defines the type of supports and resources which may be needed to foster independent living (to the greatest extent possible) past the age of 21.

Susan, our hypothetical learner with a reading disability, may need fewer post-graduation community supports than students with more severe disabilities. If Susan aspires to graduate from college, her transition plan may include the possibility that she will attend the college of her choice with her typical peers, receive tutoring services from an academic support center on campus, and be given other accommodations on testing in order to allow her to succeed. Susan would not require the same types of services other students with IEPs may need because she functions independently in all other facets of her life. This is why a transition plan is so important, because it must be tailored to the goals the student, the family, and the team have for this student post-graduation.

 ## Considerations to Ponder

As you finish reading this chapter, we encourage you to ask yourself the following questions: *Were you able to gain a new perspective on how the special education process along with the development and implementation of the IEP enables a student to receive individualized instruction according to mandates of federal law? How can you compare the special education process of today with the instructional practices of your childhood? How is it alike? How is it different? What are the implications of the special education process and IEP planning for typical learners in the 21st-century classroom? If you are a parent, how can you collaborate with the teacher to determine the best educational plan and outcome for your child using the information you have learned from this chapter?*

Conclusion

The purpose of and processes for creating IEPs grew out of everything you have read in this book thus far. Due to legal findings and subsequent regulations, it became apparent that students with special needs deserved education programs that could provide them with the same curricular access as their peers. Should schools bear the burden and hold the authority to create these educational programs alone, though?

In this chapter, you learned that parents can initiate the IEP process, just as teachers can. Also, you learned about the steps of the process and the kind of data that is collected and analyzed to create an appropriate IEP. Examples were included to make the process come alive.

While the specific steps and processes of an IEP may differ slightly from state to state or from district to district, what has been outlined here is the most accurate national description possible. The specific names of steps matter far less than the purpose of the process and the advantages that exist when it is appropriately collaborative.

Part II

Collaborating and Communicating

4

Effective Communication and Meeting Strategies

This chapter is designed to illustrate just how vital strong communication skills are to collaborative working relationships. In special education settings, we need all parties to understand each other's perspectives and to communicate effectively. Throughout this chapter, we focus on all communication elements and barriers that can lead to problems and misunderstandings. We offer advice on how to avoid these communication pitfalls, and we explain the elements of good communication in meetings.

At the root of most issues and misunderstandings is communication. We all intuitively understand this, yet very few of us spend time trying to figure out how to best avoid the problems that result from poor communication. When working with parents or advocates, the importance of effective communication becomes amplified. In fact, any time when emotions may be high, effective communication is absolutely essential.

Just think for a moment about all of the steps in effective communication. In some ways, this is analogous to a three-digit multiplication problem. Just as there are many, many opportunities in computing a three-digit multiplication problem for you to make a mistake, the same is true for communication. Forget to carry the one in multiplication, for example, and you will get the answer wrong. This is true even if you've done absolutely everything else correctly. Make a mistake in one of the communication steps, and that whole process can be messed up to. Even though we communicate all the time every day, it's important to stop and really understand the entire process.

The Communication Process

Like us, you may recall playing a game when you were a child that required one person to tell a story to another person who subsequently passed the story on to a third person. As the game progressed and the story moved from one person to the next, it became more and more distorted. At the end of the game, as we're sure you found, the story bore little resemblance to the original tale. The lesson we learned is that communication can be difficult.

Communication, too often thought of as a single act, is best understood as a complex process. The process is not complex because it challenges our cognitive abilities, but gains its complexity by virtue of the significance of each individual step, as stated earlier. Let's take a look at the different steps that make up the process (Fiore, 2016).

Idea Formation

Idea formation is the first step in the communication process. This step takes place inside your mind and involves nobody else. It is at this initial stage of communication where the speaker generates the idea he/she intends to communicate. We formulate ideas to communicate thousands of times per day. Most of them are accurate, but occasionally we may decide to communicate an idea that forms in our head that would really best be kept to ourselves. The good news is that idea formation, again, is an internal process. As a result, there is time to correct the idea before it is released to everybody else. A key to successful idea formation is to consider many alternatives and keep as open a mind as possible before settling on the appropriate idea to communicate.

Idea Encoding

Idea encoding is the process by which the idea is put into language (words and symbols) that is appropriate for conveying the intended message. Like idea formation, this step is largely internal. As such, it seems difficult to imagine any problem with this step. The truth is, however, that many communication problems have their roots deeply planted in idea encoding. We often know what we want to communicate, but we may choose words that fail to communicate it as effectively as we would have hoped. The opportunities for communication breakdown are great at this stage. The way in which an idea is encoded, therefore, is vitally important to the success of any communication process.

Communication Channel

The method by which an individual communicates an idea is referred to as the communication channel. A message may be delivered in writing, which would clearly only allow for one-way communication. A message could also be delivered verbally, either to an individual or a group. Messages often-times are also delivered via telephone, text message, or email. Each of these is a communication channel. Sometimes, the biggest mistake we make when communicating is with the channel. Certain messages are best delivered via certain channels. Typically, for example, challenging news is best delivered face-to-face. Choosing to send something that is sensitive via text message is not necessarily the best channel for communication in some cases.

Receiver Decoding

The final step in the communication process is called receiver decoding. At this point, the responsibility for communication has temporarily shifted from the individual who originated the thought to the person who is receiving the information. It is at this stage that problems are encountered time and time again. If you have ever been in a situation where you thought you said one thing, but people heard something different, then you may have experienced a breakdown in receiver decoding. Because receiver decoding does not take place internal to the person who originated the idea, it is difficult for that person to control. I may consider my idea very carefully. I may choose the most appropriate words and symbols for communicating it, as well. Finally, the communication channel I use might be the best one in this circumstance and might afford you the best opportunity to ask for clarification. If, however, you do not perceive my message in the way I intended, then a communication breakdown beyond my control will have occurred. This can be extremely frus-trating, and can lead to accusations such as "You weren't listening to what I said." These accusations, as we know, are often incorrect. Oftentimes, people really do listen, but they simply interpret the message differently than the way in which it was intended. There are many factors that affect whether or not receiver decoding is accurate, as intended. Although the most obvious factors are within our control (idea formation, idea encoding, communication channel), there are others that are far more difficult to plan for. There may be a language barrier, a cultural difference, a difference in the reading level if the message was sent in writing, or a temporarily poor attitude on the part of the receiver.

There are, as mentioned, so many opportunities for miscommunication to occur anywhere along the continuum of the communication process. If our goal is to develop and nurture positive communication with all stakeholders within the school community, then we must understand this process and constantly examine our effectiveness in using it. We will not eliminate all communication breakdowns. We can, however, minimize them by paying attention to the pro-cess and understanding the specifics of how breakdowns in communication typically occur.

Nonverbal Communication

Communicating effectively would be so much easier if communication problems were limited to the ideas we have and the words we choose to transmit our idea. If only we needed to concern ourselves solely with the words we choose and the way in which we choose to use them, there would be far fewer communication breakdowns. Unfortunately, that is almost never the case. We communicate so many of our ideas without ever saying a word. Instead, a substantial amount of what we communicate comes through nonverbal behaviors and the information those behaviors give others about how we truly are feeling. Our nonverbal communication is often far more powerful than our verbal communication. This is particularly true when there is a perceived mismatch between the words we are saying and the nonverbal reactions we are indicating.

Say, for instance, you and I are engaged in an important conversation and I observe that you are sitting with your arms tightly folded across your chest. I also notice that your legs are tightly crossed, and I become a bit uneasy. To myself, I begin examining the nature of our conversation. Am I upsetting you? Have the words I have chosen to communicate offended you in some way? Are you unwilling to speak with me, and would you have preferred that I wrote you a note or called you on your cell phone to have this conversation? Is there something wrong with you that has caused you to misinterpret what I am saying?

All of these questions race through my mind because of my perception of your nonverbal communication. Your arms tightly folded and legs tightly crossed tell me that you are angry or unreceptive to what I am saying. Although it certainly was not my intent to do so, I become absolutely certain that I have somehow offended or bothered you. Not being able to stand it any longer, I ask you what I have done and why you are upset. When you reply that you are not at all upset, I inform you of the negative vibes I am picking up from your body language, or nonverbal communication. Your reply to me is simple: "Well, it's freezing cold in here." Imagine the snowball effect that might have taken place if I had been uncomfortable or unwilling to confront my perceptions of your nonverbal behavior. This sort of misunderstanding routinely occurs in our interactions with others, and it is exacerbated in emotional situations.

There are probably as many incorrect interpretations of nonverbal communication as there are correct ones. In the above example, while it is true that tightly crossed arms and legs often signify resistance, anger, or being upset, they can also signify being cold. Of course, there are other examples of nonverbal communication that we tend to associate with particular feelings or attitudes. It is vital that we remember, though, that the exhibition of a certain behavior does not necessarily mean that we have the associated attitudes or feelings at the moment we are gesturing.

For this reason, it is wise for anybody concerned with accurate communication to be conscious of their own nonverbal behaviors as well as the nonverbal behaviors of others. These behaviors can be misleading, though. People really do cross their arms from time to time to signify that they are feeling cold. Some individuals swallow frequently not because they are nervous, but because they have a sore throat.

When you think about the words we use and the nonverbal messages we give, it becomes easy to understand that there are so many opportunities for communication breakdowns or miscommunication to occur. In fact, sometimes it feels as though it is easier to miscommunicate than it is to communicate effectively. Beyond the words and nonverbal cues we give when we communicate a message to somebody, there are other meaningful barriers for certain segments of our population. Parents or other advocates may misunderstand what we are trying to communicate if any of the following barriers are present.

Language Barriers

Language barriers to communication were far less significant a few decades ago than they are today. This is due to the fact that an increasingly large number of families with children in our schools do not speak or read English at a level of functional literacy. In fact, recent estimates are that English is not the primary language spoken in somewhere between 20 and 25 percent of American homes. Children from homes in which English is never spoken or is spoken as a secondary language represent one of the fastest-growing segments of our school populations. This is true in almost all areas of the United States. The parents of these children must be communicated with just like the parents of English-speaking children. They have the same legal rights, and they have the same moral rights. It is imperative that these parents and advocates have opportunities to fully understand and participate in the Individualized Education Plan (IEP) process.

Cultural Barriers

It is imperative that all educators recognize the different cultural interpretations of body language and space since so much communication takes place nonverbally. We are reminded here of an exhibit that we once saw in a museum. This exhibit was designed to illustrate the differences that exist in spatial proximity between communicants in various cultures. By standing on footprints strategically placed on the floor of this exhibit, two people could mimic the distance that would be customary to have between them during a conversation if they were from different cultures. This illustrated the fact that people clearly differ in their tolerance for personal space; some prefer very close communication distances, whereas others prefer greater distances.

Another point to consider is the cultural differences noted in whether or not individuals gaze into a speaker's eyes when they are listening to him/her. Anglos are socialized to gaze directly at the speaker's face when they are listening; Japanese-Americans avoid eye contact when listening by focusing on the speaker's neck, so as not to appear rude; African-Americans and Native Americans rarely look directly into the eyes of an authority figure. These cultural differences must be appreciated so that none of us misinterpret them. Otherwise, unnecessary barriers to effective communication are created.

Physical Barriers

An often forgotten and frequently underrepresented group of stakeholders are those individuals with physical disabilities. Dependent upon the limitations of the individual, their communication requirements may be the same as individuals without disabilities, or they may be profoundly different. Think, for example, of a person who is legally blind. This individual will not be able to pick up on subtle facial gestures to the same degree as a person who is not blind. Consequently, all educators must be sensitive to the degree to which their messages are typically delivered through facial gestures. Along these same lines, consider the limitations that might face a person who relies on lip reading to "hear" what is being communicated. It may be that this person is a better "listener" than somebody who has full use of his/her ears for this purpose. It also may be, however, that the rate at which we speak should be altered for this individual. The important thing to remember is that we all need to be aware of the limitations. We all need to believe that communication issues make all important events, such as an IEP meeting, much more difficult than they need to be.

Finally, please don't think that barriers are insurmountable. Instead, enter into any important communication setting with an understanding that barriers to effective communication are everywhere. As long as you notice them with a keen eye, you can eliminate them with relative ease.

Perception Checking

Consider the earlier example of our fictitious conversation in which you had your arms tightly folded across your chest. Remember how, in the hypothetical situation described earlier, I was unnerved by your body language? Recall, if you will, the struggle I had in understanding just what it was I said that offended you. Most importantly, remember how incorrect my assumption about your body language was. You were not angry or unwilling to listen. You were, in fact, cold.

Had I checked my perception of your body language with you, I could have avoided a great deal of my confusion and concern regarding your feelings. I could have found out early on that you were not unhappy with me, but were instead cold.

Using the skill of perception checking requires that you ask the person you are communicating with whether or not you are correctly perceiving their feelings. It does not imply any judgment of these feelings, but rather affords you an opportunity to see if you have perceived them correctly. In our example, it would sound something like this: "I notice that you are crossing your arms. Are you unhappy with something I said?" Your reply would have been simple: "No, I'm just cold." Failure to use perception checking may have led to a conversation sounding more like this: "When you sit there with your arms folded and your angry, closed-minded attitude, I just can't continue this meeting." The very same nonverbal cue, having not been perception-checked, could destroy a meeting or a relationship.

Using the skill of perception checking is easy and, if done regularly and consistently, it can become a useful habit rather quickly. Instead of mistaking somebody's nonverbal cues for a feeling that is not present, you easily can be in a position to read other people's emotions in no time at all. Also, if you check your perception, you often may find that it is right on target. For example, you might see somebody with their arms crossed, assume they are angry, check your perception by asking them, and then have them tell you that you are correct. They are, in fact, angry! Whether your perception is correct or not is not the issue. Once you check your perception with the other person, you will understand how they are feeling. It is always easier to communicate with somebody when you know how they feel and where you stand with them.

So how does this affect an important meeting like an IEP conference? First, it helps ensure that you or the meeting facilitator know how everybody is feeling before you start. Second, when you are delivering information or explaining a strategy, it gives you the opportunity to best understand how your explanation is being perceived. Oftentimes, we adjust our message slightly in response to another person's reaction. This is an invaluable communication skill, and it's a whole lot easier to do if you understand the reaction completely.

Communication Strategies for Meetings

Strong communication skills almost always lead to successful meetings in a team atmosphere. Between the two of us, we have been to scores of IEP meetings. We have seen them run successfully, with open, honest communication, and we have seen them run poorly, where every attendee felt tension and a sense of conflict. In each instance where the meeting was a positive one, there was strong and effective communication being modeled by the meeting facilitator. Also, there was a strong sense of team. Although the attendees, specifically teacher(s), parent(s), and advocate(s), are seen as adversaries in the negative and poorly run meetings, they are collaborators and teammates when meetings are run well.

Admittedly, much of the success occurs when parents, advocates, and teachers are, and feel like, obvious teammates due to the overall positive culture of the school. We know that in schools with positive cultures, people get along, pull together, and share common goals. Also, we know that it takes time and deliberation to improve the culture of a school. Positive and effective communication is one of the most important tools to improve a school's culture. However, even when the culture is not as positive as we may want it to be, strong and effective communication skills at a meeting go very far in ensuring that people at the meeting think and function as a team in that particular setting.

What follow are some general meeting guidelines that make meeting time more effective and lead to minimized conflict scenarios.

These are simple methods that highlight ways that meeting facilitators can guide participants in thoughtful and effective communication. Use these strategies in all of your IEP meetings, and you will be amazed at how improved communication skills lead to better teamwork, increased morale, and more successful meetings!

1. Outline Meeting Goals and Expectations at the Onset
Begin the meeting by outlining overall meeting objectives and what the intended outcome is (an actionable IEP, for example). By stating upfront what you plan to achieve, the likelihood is increased that all participants will remain focused. If things get off track, which often occurs when talking about students, their learning goals, and their behavioral goals, refer everyone back to the meeting's goals and purpose. If any secondary topics come up, you can always make note of them and return to them later.

2. Foster Listening (and Understanding) among Attendees
Sometimes people miss out on valuable questions, perspectives, and ideas because they're too focused on making their own points or advancing their own

agendas. Help deter that by actively giving everyone a chance to speak, and then by making sure that everyone else at the meeting is paying full attention. If it appears there is any miscommunication, take a moment to let people repeat their statements or follow up with additional information. The most important thing is to model this consistently. With all of the distractions that exist in our world today, it is vital that you do everything you can to remain focused and attentive.

3. Answer All Questions and Make All Statements with Honesty

Asking a question in front of a group can be embarrassing or intimidating, especially for parents or advocates who don't spend every day at the school. Some may fear that their question is silly or that they are the only one with that particular question. As long as people feel that way, there is an increased chance that critical concerns will go unaddressed. Therefore, explain that all questions are good questions, give honest answers, and make people feel good about raising their concern or seeking the clarification they need. Similarly, you need to respond to questions thoroughly and honestly, and you need to confirm with everybody that what you've explained makes sense to them. In short, you need to check your perceptions of others' understanding.

4. Be Respectful of Others' Ideas

It would be silly to assume that anybody attending the meeting has no important information or ideas to contribute, since people do come to IEP meetings with ideas, hopes, and thoughts. Even with individual goals or agendas, conflict may be inevitable. So, right at the beginning of the meeting, make it clear that while people are free to disagree, they must do so courteously. Model this courtesy, and ensure that everybody knows the meeting is a safe place to disagree.

5. Celebrate Once a Decision Has Been Reached, or a Plan Has Been Outlined

Reaching your meeting's goal and developing, improving, modifying, or concluding an IEP is worth celebrating. As such, each participant should feel good about what has been accomplished. It is important to highlight individual accomplishments and team members who went the extra mile, either in preparation for the meeting or during the meeting. Furthermore, it's important to highlight all positive examples of collaborations and teamwork that led to the successful meeting accomplishments.

 ## Considerations to Ponder

A part of the job that many teachers abhor is the meetings they must attend. Whether they are faculty meetings, grade level meetings, district meetings, or even IEP meetings, meetings are universally disliked. Is it possible that this universal dislike of meetings occurs because the meetings aren't run well? Is it possible that communication barriers or breakdowns lead to meetings that teachers find to be unproductive and unfulfilling?

While our focus is most specifically on IEP meetings, take the knowledge you have about successful communication and meeting strategies with you to your next meeting. As you exhibit appropriate communication behaviors, others may begin to as well. Maybe meetings finally can become productive and fulfilling.

Conclusion

Remember, these are general guidelines, but the underlying principle is actually profound. In meetings that involve anything emotional or potentially contentious, the friendlier and more open you are, the better. Oftentimes, these meetings can feel stifling and overly formal. It is the exact opposite climate that we ought to create. Conflict always declines and productivity always increases when the meeting environment is lighter and more friendly.

In most school districts, there are specific processes that must be followed in IEP meetings. While these processes likely dictate who leads the meeting and the order of events that should unfold, there is still room for any and all participants to be expert communicators and facilitators. Even if the meeting structure has you only reporting a specific piece of information at a specific time, your communication skills are utilized from the moment you walk in the door. You have the power to make people feel welcome, you can demonstrate through your smile and eye contact that the meeting is a safe, non-threatening environment, and you can validate people's opinions and feelings through positive and open nonverbal communication.

5

"Rule of Three"
Working with Professional Advocates

In this chapter, we explain the "Rule of Three" and ensure that an appreciation can be gained of the valuable roles of the teacher, the parent, and the advocate. When we think of all three as a team and eliminate thinking of conflict, it becomes easier to recognize that the role of an advocate is not to take sides. An advocate is there to help ensure that the child's educational needs are met. Advocates are completely on our side *if* we all are on the side of the child. The many examples in this chapter should spark some thinking and draw some parallels to situations that you know very well.

Today, in the 21st-century classroom, students are learning in new and exciting ways, and teachers are using data, measured accurately and often, to drive instruction. The focus has shifted from group learning to individualized and small group instruction using multi-faceted pedagogical methods, environments, and delivery models. With the advent of the co-teaching model, it is not uncommon to have two or three teachers in a classroom simultaneously instructing heterogeneous groups of learners on one lesson. A heterogeneous group is a group comprised of students who may differ slightly in their ability levels, but still share at least one thing in common, such as their learning style, which can be auditory (listening), visual (viewing), or kinesthetic (moving). Each group may be learning the same content, with the same Common Core Standard (the national standards for English language arts, literacy, and math, broken down into small, measurable objectives), but the material used to teach and understand the content may differ according to the needs of the learners.

Now, as you think about your early elementary education days, take a moment and imagine your classroom. Was it designed to enable you to learn the way you learn best, or was it set up for the convenience of the teacher? Picture your desk. We are sure it was neatly situated in a row, which started from the front of the room going in a straight line to the back of the room. Why do you think it was designed that way? Was it for you? Or was it so the teacher could easily maneuver between the rows to monitor student learning after instruction had been delivered. Now, imagine a new way of learning. If you peek inside a 21st-century third grade classroom, it looks very different than what you experienced. The chalkboard is no longer in the front of the room. There is often more than one adult in the room, and the students are divided into groups. Below, we will give you a vivid description of a typical lesson in today's classroom and how it might look to an observer. Pay special attention to the learning environment and how it differs from what you experienced. Then think about how this type of classroom setup impacts the way students interact with teachers today. Reflect on the concept of Universal Design for Learning. Is the modern classroom you are about to picture universally designed for all learners?

Envisioning the 21st-Century Classroom

Imagine a small group of third graders today, working at a kidney-shaped table with the teacher in the center. Behind the teacher is a movable whiteboard, where the teacher and/or the students can draw or write as they are progressing through the lesson. The students are all typical for their age and development, but they all are all visual learners, so their favorite thing to do is draw. These students enjoy talking and interacting with their peers, but when they get in a large group, they sometimes lose focus, so the small group keeps them engaged and excited to participate. Now, as the students interact with the teacher, the teacher personalizes the learning for each student, giving positive, specific feedback like, "I love the way you explained the meaning of the word 'summit' to the group. Can you draw a picture of a 'summit' on the whiteboard to show what the meaning of the word is, too?" In order to evaluate students as they are learning, the teacher then uses a checklist to measure whether or not the student can understand and explain the concept. The students cannot see what the teacher is writing, but the teacher is gathering formative data on what he/she sees the students may or may not understand about the new vocabulary word. The students are all on task, and they are learning in a way that suits

their specific needs. This is relevant learning, because the students can participate; therefore, it is in these students' Zone of Proximal Development. How
did you feel when you read this lesson? Did you, as a student learn this way?
Did the teacher's personal, small-group approach make you want to join in?

Now, imagine in the same room James and Mike, two rambunctious, creative, and gifted third graders. They hate working in groups because they feel
like other students bother them or interrupt their thinking too much. Their
vocabulary knowledge is well beyond that of a typical third grader, and
their ability to read and interpret text is at a fifth grade level. James and Mike
would be bored working in a group on a simple vocabulary lesson, so they
are working on an independent learning contract. James and Mike each sit
at a desk on opposite sides of the room in a study carrel with a laptop. They
look up their vocabulary words using an online dictionary, log in to a writing
application on their laptops, and begin to write an informative essay. James
loves snakes, so his story must utilize all seven of his vocabulary words. It
must have a great topic sentence, six descriptive sentences which relate to his
topic sentence, and a solid conclusion which restates in a different way what
the topic sentence discussed. Mike enjoys motorcycles. Instead of doing a writing assignment like James, though, he is given a learning contract where he is
completing an informational blog for other students to read. His assignment
has the same learning criterion that James has, but his writing assignment is
slightly differentiated to accommodate his interests and needs. This motivates
him intrinsically, which means he feels the desire to complete the assignment
without any outside reward. He just enjoys doing it because it is fun for him.

These are just two short examples of what 21st-century learning looks like.
If you entered any elementary school today in any part of the United States,
public or private, it would look similar to what we just described above. The
only thing that would be different is the number of students, the number of
teachers, the type of content, and the type of groupings. Otherwise, teaching
has become very individualized, which has allowed students to work more
independently and more creatively, and to develop greater technology skills.
This will serve students well into the next twenty years or so as they work to
reach their potential by giving them the type of instruction they really need
to be active participants in their learning, and to provide them an opportunity to
really get to know their teachers, their peers, and, more importantly, themselves.

Instructional Implications

As you can see, teaching really has evolved from being an art to being both an
art *and* a science. Teachers are expected to understand more and more about

the brain, how it works, and the many biological and environmental factors affecting learning. The implication for this type of change in instruction means that having only one teacher plan to deliver and assess the lesson for all learners is not conducive to highly differentiated and universal teaching. Teaching collaboratively today involves using a whole group of experts – regular education teachers, special education teachers, psychologists, reading specialists, speech therapists, guidance counselors, technology teachers, and other professionals. Planning, executing, and examining the outcome of each lesson and the implication for each learner is now facilitated both throughout and beyond the school day. Teams can be comprised of a variety of different experts. Vertical teams (such as third through sixth grade science teachers) or horizontal teams (all third grade team members in a district) can plan together on a weekly, monthly, or quarterly basis. These horizontal and vertical teams can also partner with special education teams and other service providers to accommodate specific learning needs of the exceptional learners. More time is spent co-planning, co-teaching, and evaluating a lesson than ever before. Data from both formal (completed in a written format, such as a test, a written assignment, or a group project) and informal (simple anecdotal observation of a student's participation in class lessons, discussions, or assessments) sources is analyzed by the team, and then future instruction is provided according to the results of the data. As the team uses data to drive instruction, input must be gleaned from parent(s) and any other outside sources as well. Teaching is no longer a lonely profession, but rather a profession of tremendous interdependence. Today's teacher must rely upon, analyze, and use the data collected from all those who influence how the child learns, behaves, and interacts with others on a daily basis.

Considerations to Ponder

When we started our teaching careers, vertical teams and horizontal teams actually represented new concepts. The evolution of instructional planning and the collaborations between and among teachers are relatively new in our schools. However, for many readers, *not* planning and collaborating with other teachers, whether at your own grade level or not, is a normal and essential part of your work.

Working collaboratively with parents and advocates, sadly, is similar to vertical and horizontal teams. That is, successfully collaborating with adults who are not teachers is relatively new in our schools. At least, doing it well is new. You have the skills to improve the lives of your students with special needs, and you have the knowledge and disposition to involve parents and advocates successfully in the process.

"Rule of Three"

As you study how the context for learning has evolved from when you attended elementary and middle school, you will also develop a greater understanding of how 21st-century learning demands from those who support students in the classroom are changing. Educators and parents can and should utilize advocates to help bridge the gap between home and school. This is called the "Rule of Three". The "Rule of Three" consists of the parent(s), the teacher, and the advocate working together to develop an ongoing, trust-based, data-driven relationship that builds success for the student (Figure 5.1). Research shows that teachers and parents work more effectively together if an objective third party (advocate) is present and available to "mediate" meetings, represent parent concerns and perspectives, and clarify instructional implications for the student to the parent as the school year progresses. Partnering in a team of three allows objective data to drive decision-making while still creating a forum for opinion-sharing and empathetic understanding for the student and his/her family. As you continue to read this chapter, you will not only learn the role of each member of this three-person team, but you will also learn strategies on how to make the team successful. The first member of the

Figure 5.1 The Three Important Members of the Individualized Education Plan (IEP) Process

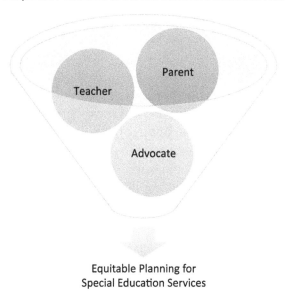

Equitable Planning for
Special Education Services

team we will consider is the parent. Parents are an integral part of student success when it comes to language acquisition, communication, and data sharing, as the next section of this chapter will explain.

Parents: Partners in Language, Communication, and Data Collection

Parents are an integral part of student success across the curriculum. However, the most important part of how parents influence learning is language acquisition. Much of what students acquire occurs in and around the home during the first few years of life. Research shows that preschool children are biologically inclined to acquire language through experiences of sight and sound. If a child is raised in a home where the use of language (from any culture) is limited, the child will have limited language development. This creates a context of deficiency in language acquisition. Developing a child's language ability requires tremendous partnership between the home and the school, and must be created in such a way that the instruction is both relevant and deliberate for the child. Lev Vygotsky (1962, p. 108) suggests that the communication connections do not have to take place immediately, but that "in the course of further schoolwork and reading", learners can make the association between concepts and experience. Vygotsky describes the teacher's role as assisting students in the recognition of decontextualized, systematic concepts. Symbolism, through the use of images (stop signs) and sounds connected with traffic, media, and other public displays, enhances a child's ability to make associations, build sound/symbol relationships, and form language rules. In time, the way the child observes and acquires language becomes the foundation for the way the child perceives the world.

Take a moment and picture yourself as a child at home with your parent(s). Think about what kind of language was spoken. Did your parents speak to you in full sentences, with proper grammar, or did they speak to you in sentences full of slang? Did you learn to speak one language, or multiple languages? How much did you travel, and how many books did your parents read to you as a child? All of these things affect the way you learned language.

As you think about your language exposure and the way your parents encouraged your language development as a child, think of the students with whom you may work and the implications for instruction based on their different backgrounds and language needs. Below you will see two examples of two different students who need special education services. As you read their stories, imagine how important parental involvement may be in their acquisition of language. Think about what questions you may have for each parent as you read. How would you build a rapport with each family and develop a plan to help the student be successful based on many different factors: culture, language, socio-economic status, and so on?

First, we would like to tell you about "Juan". Juan is a sweet, gentle young man from a Hispanic family. His family moved to Hays, Kansas from Puerto Rico about one year ago. Juan is entering first grade. Juan's father is a laborer, and he spends his days on farms, harvesting wheat. Juan's father quit school in fifth grade to help support his family back in Puerto Rico. His native language is Spanish, and he speaks it fluently, but he writes very poorly. Juan's father also does not speak English, nor write it. He is beginning to recognize symbols and words around him, but when he speaks to Juan, he only speaks to him in Spanish. Juan has had no exposure to the English language other than what he has seen in brief television shows or on signs. He is starting first grade with a severe English language deficit in both reading and writing. Although he is not cognitively delayed based on testing done by the school psychologist, he will need complete language immersion in the classroom in addition to an English as a Second Language (ESL) teacher in order for him to learn and develop appropriate language skills on a par with his typically developing American peers. Juan's parents will need tremendous support as Juan receives his education. Not only will there be significant differences in how he will acclimate to the American way of life culturally, but there will be huge barriers to his social relationships and his academic growth, since he has little or no experience of conversing with American children his age. What are the implications for Juan's education? Who will help you build a rapport with his family when they only speak Spanish? What if his parents have a negative perspective of education and do not want to help Juan learn? How will you help them understand your goals and ideas to enable Juan to learn and grow in your class?

Now, let's think about a completely different type of student who is an exceptional learner. Meet "James". James is a black youth who hails from the north side of Chicago. James is the son of a pediatrician in West Town. Both of his parents are educated and well traveled. James attended a private Catholic school during his elementary education and will now be attending public middle school as he enters the sixth grade. He is a bright, but highly distracted, youth who ended up in the principal's office too often. His parents grew tired of his attention issues, but also knew he was bored and needed a change. James reads and writes at an eighth grade level and has been recommended for the gifted program by his previous teachers. James's parents have asked what type of educational and reading programs are available from the public school he will attend to support his learning. They are tired of the strict religious, authoritarian style of teaching many Catholic schools provide, and they want him to be able to learn with students from diverse backgrounds, but they are going to monitor his education closely to make sure the law is followed. They both want to make sure that James is challenged, since he tends to get distracted if he gets bored. Since James's dad is a pediatrician and his mother is the owner of a small business, they are both incredibly busy. The Intervention Specialist where James will go to school happens to be licensed to work with gifted students in addition to students with special needs, which will serve James well. James's parents really want to understand how best they can work with the school to ensure he will be successful as he transitions from private school to public school. They have no idea how to ask for what James needs, but they are very sure that they will hold the school accountable for meeting James's academic, social, and emotional needs during the school day.

What are the educational implications for an exceptional learner like James in reading and writing? How will you challenge him? How will you work with his parents knowing that they are already feeling angry and frustrated with his previous educational experience? How can you ensure that everything you are doing as an educator complies with the law, but gives James everything he needs to reach his academic, social, and emotional potential in this new, particularly difficult, environment?

Learning about your students' families, their cultures, and their language development is just a small part of navigating through the teaching maze. It doesn't matter whether you are a regular education teacher or a special education teacher. The first critical role of the teacher is to build a trust rapport with the parent. This is the most valuable part as you work to implement the "Rule of Three". Developing a trust rapport will build a sense of community, open lines of communication, and help to bridge the gap between what is being implemented at school and what is being taught at home. As stated in the previous chapter, teaching is no longer a lonely profession; it is a profession of collaborators, working together for the needs of each child.

In order to begin an open line of communication, the teacher needs to create a safe, positive environment for the parent(s) to share ideas and input on the student's education. This starts before the school year even begins. Parents really want to know that the teacher cares. After all, parents are entrusting teachers with their most precious treasure, their child. As we think back to one important example from our early parenting years, we remember the year our youngest son entered first grade. This was a pivotal year, because it set the tone for communication between home and school for years to come in our family. The trust rapport that was built between the teacher and both of us that year taught us that it was equally important for us to be involved in the educational activities of our child as it was for the teacher. The teacher needed us, and we needed the teacher.

Before school started, during orientation, the teacher gave each parent a little notebook with a pen attached. We won't sugar-coat things by saying Nicholas was a bright little angelic young man who never disobeyed us. In fact, he was bright little man, but he was also difficult at times. As the year progressed, the notebook the teacher gave us provided insight into an important problem that surfaced every day. Through the daily communication in his notebook, we would learn that Nicholas spent most recesses "on the wall", which meant standing, facing a wall, without permission to interact with his peers, for various little offenses he had committed during the day. During parent–teacher conferences, the physical education teacher commented that he thought Nicholas would spend his life "on the wall". We chuckled, but we were worried, surprised, and certainly disappointed at that comment. We both wondered how taking away the recess of a very active, curious, and precocious child could benefit his academic and social needs. It was because of that daily notebook that we were prompted to ask for clarification regarding the "on the wall" situation with Nick. We both reached out to the teacher by writing in the notebook, and the teacher called us in to meet with her. Together, we discussed Nick's daily offenses, his behaviors at home, how we would partner to hold Nick accountable, and how we could both prevent Nick from fulfilling the physical education teacher's prophecy of spending his life "on the wall" with no chance for parole. It was in that daily communication that we both felt "safe" to share our feelings, our concerns, and develop our combined plan of action. It was personal, meaningful, and purposeful. It also provided a continuum of service from home to school. Nicholas was being cared for the way a community should care for a child; with love, consistent expectations, and shared responsibility. The evidence of his behavior changes as the year progressed showed that good communication builds trust – and the opportunity to solve problems. Nicholas spent far fewer recesses "on the wall" after that meeting, the meeting that began because of a notebook. It was simple, but it was powerful.

After a teacher develops a keen awareness of his/her students' language abilities, creates and implements a forum for communication, and establishes a trust rapport with the family, the next job is for the teacher to begin to learn to partner with the parent to collect the data necessary to drive instruction. This is the tricky part, because the data can be observed and collected in different ways, yielding inconsistent results. While a good trust rapport and an open line of communication are both critical in creating a personalized relationship between the family and the school, the difficult part is when that trust rapport is challenged by the inability of the parent/teacher partnership to view data objectively.

Advocate: Mediator, Negotiator, and Objective Third Party

This is where the importance of the Special Education Advocate comes into play. (For simplicity, the Special Education Advocate will be referred to as just the "advocate" hereafter.) The advocate is crucial to the success of the parent/teacher team in that he/she serves as the mediator between the two parties when an objective decision cannot be made. After all, both parties are heavily invested in the success of the student. We both believe that neither the parent nor the teacher intend to be subjective when collecting, analyzing, and reporting data, but it does happen. When one spends hours per day providing personalized care, it is hard not to develop a subjective viewpoint.

The narrative we have written below exemplifies why the role of the advocate was developed, how it helps both the parent and the teacher, and how the real purpose of the advocate is not to take a "side", but to speak for the child, who may be too young or incapable of having a voice. You will see in this example that the advocate is, at times, the voice for the parent, the voice for the teacher, and most importantly, the voice for the child. There is an old adage, "There are two sides to every story." We believe there are actually three: the teacher, the parent, and the child. The advocate speaks for the child while helping to enforce the law, so that busy teachers and administrators can ensure they are doing everything possible to implement the best education. When districts are overwhelmed with students who have special needs, the role of the advocate can be so valuable, as it assists in analyzing the data, reporting the data, and following up on communication between the parent and the school. The advocate is also a legal advisor, holding both the school and the family accountable. This is why we believe in firmly applying the "Rule of Three" in many special education cases. Someone must represent the needs of the child as often as possible. The advocate, when trained properly, is the person to do so. This is protective for both the school and the family. It also ensures the neutrality that is so vital for what can be intense conversations involving emotions of all parties present.

The example we are about to give is provided for both parents and teachers. This is not an example of "persuasiveness", but of "perspective". As both educators and parents, our most important role is to develop "perspective" and create empathy for one another. It is not to be convinced of one another's viewpoint, but to simply acknowledge one another's viewpoint, to respect it, and to work with it, so that something purposeful and powerful might occur: collaboration. We've all been in positions when it was difficult, if not impossible, to see an opposing viewpoint. After all, the reason we feel so passionate about what we do, as a parent or as an educator, is because we care. If we didn't care, there would be no reason to argue. We would simply give in, agree, and move on. Thankfully, on both sides of this story, you'll find that the teacher and the parent both truly care. As you read, be sure to keep that in mind. It will help you when you want to step in and take a side. Whether you are a parent or a teacher, you will begin to gain new insight as to why advocacy is so critical, and why the "Rule of Three" is truly essential in 21st-century learning. Public education is changing, at both state and federal levels. We believe, more than ever before, that we need advocates.

Let us introduce "Rebecca". Rebecca is an eighth grade student who has been identified as having a severe learning disability in reading. Rebecca is social and athletic. She enjoys participating in a variety of peer-related groups, which include church, horse-back riding, and swimming. She is talkative and friendly when she is around her same-age peers in social settings where she feels confident in her abilities. However, in school, you will often find Rebecca withdrawing from interactions with her peers in academic-related activities. She tries very hard to exclude herself, because she feels certain that everyone around her can sense that she is struggling to read. She is embarrassed, sullen, and rarely completes assignments on time.

Rebecca goes home each day and tells her parents how frustrated she is with her teachers. She says they try to draw attention to her in class by offering to help her. She wishes they would just "leave her alone". She likes to work with one or two classmates with whom she feels safe. When her teachers try to pair her up with other classmates who may have similar interests, but different abilities, Rebecca refuses and claims that her teachers really don't know what she needs. If they knew what was best for her, they would let her work with the same students every day. She is tired of being embarrassed by her teachers.

Rebecca's parents spend a lot of time contacting the school principal on behalf of Rebecca. Both parents work full-time jobs, so they feel that the responsibility for Rebecca's education falls primarily with the school. They cannot tell what is wrong with Rebecca's learning, but they know she is several levels behind her typical peers in reading. The school principal is quick to defend the teachers, knowing that the classrooms are full of students who have a wide variety of learning styles and needs. The principal feels that Rebecca, being about to enter high school, needs to take more responsibility for her own learning. However, the principal has to hear both sides of the story, so has meetings whenever Rebecca's parents request them in order to make them happy. Rebecca's parents are tired of being in meetings where promises are made to help Rebecca, but no plans are actually developed with follow-through. Rebecca's parents feel that the team of teachers and administrators simply hand out a bunch of papers with some numbers on it and talk in a language they do not understand. They are always nice and polite to the family, but then nothing changes.

When you read this story, were you able to see the parent perspective? Did you understand how frustrating it was for the parents to hear their child's needs weren't being met at school? Did you feel empathy for the fact that the language used by the team of teachers and administrators was too difficult to understand and that no plans were made with follow-through to help Rebecca? Did it make you angry? What would you do if you were Rebecca's parents?

As you were gaining perspective on the parent role in the "Rule of Three" in Rebecca's story, you may have noticed that you began to "side" with the family. After all, the parents do have a valid point that Rebecca's needs are not being met by the school team. There is little objective and/or anecdotal evidence to prove that the meetings which are taking place ensure Rebecca's voice is heard and the parents' concerns are addressed. While this may seem true in Rebecca's circumstances, it isn't true in all situations regarding special education in public schools. Many public schools are very diligent about providing frequent evidence and action plans relevant to student needs. However, for those districts where time, resources, and problem-solving are difficult to manage in the ever-changing educational climate, advocacy can be the answer to both the parent perspective and the school perspective, because it serves to connect both parties by providing a non-judgmental, objective viewpoint, which assists in communicating, in a fair and equitable manner, both parent and school needs.

In the next section, you will see how utilizing an advocate can help take the pressure off parents while ensuring the school team is following the law and consistently communicating the procedures and safeguards in place to assist the student in the educational process. You will discover how the 21st-century educational team is truly an interactive and collaborative force. You will also learn how no teacher, no matter how skilled, educated, or experienced, should be left to fend on his/her own in important legal matters. Teachers are working harder than ever to take care of the needs of a wide variety of students in the most demanding educational climate in the history of education. Parents need teachers, and teachers need parents. They both need support.

"Rule of Three": Teacher, Parent, and Advocate

You may remember Chapter 3, where it was mentioned that teachers are no longer "islands". Today, teachers are constantly gathering input from a variety of professional colleagues to gauge their students' progress on a daily basis. If you are a teacher, you may be able to identify easily with the following scenario in a public school setting today.

You've read about the parent's perspective, but for now, let's analyze things from a teacher's perspective, so that you can visualize how inter-dependent teaching has become. It's Tuesday at 10 a.m. at "Pioneer Middle School". Even though the school day doesn't officially begin until 7:45 a.m., the teacher, Ms. Martin, has been at work since 6:30 a.m., preparing for an IEP meeting, co-planning with her sixth grade team, and finishing her lessons for the day. She is currently in a classroom of twenty-five sixth graders, teaching a small group of students with different abilities a lesson in fractions. The sixth grade math teacher is sitting on the opposite side of the room with a larger group, instructing the same lesson, using slightly different materials and moving at a faster pace. Ms. Martin has an electronic tablet in her lap as she sits on the floor, handing each student fraction cards to sort equivalent fractions. As she interacts with each student, she records, through the use of a checklist, the student's knowledge of the content she teaches. In the middle of the lesson, one of the students in Ms. Martin's group becomes agitated. He refuses to work, gets up, and leaves the room, and the entire class becomes distracted. Ms. Martin has several decisions to make. She must ensure that the students she is teaching continue their lesson. She must also ensure the student who left the room will not harm himself or others. In addition to this, Ms. Martin is no longer able to collect data on the remaining students in the group.

As this scenario developed, keep in mind that in less than two minutes Ms. Martin made a decision based on one student's behavior which cascaded into involving the cooperation and coordination of services from various pro-fessional colleagues in the school. She communicated via walkie-talkie with the secretary in the office that the student was agitated, had left the classroom, and was now roaming the halls. The secretary followed up on that communi-cation in the office by notifying the Dean of Students that an agitated student had left the classroom. The Dean of Students then reached out to the school psychologist to meet with Ms. Martin as soon as the student was found in the hallway. Ms. Martin knew she must then also communicate the follow-up information on this student to the entire sixth grade team of teachers in order to facilitate a plan of action to prevent future emotional outbursts from the student. Ms. Martin is feeling overwhelmed. She knows that this student is in crisis. She also knows the protocols and procedures that must take place in order to assist the student; however, she cannot do it alone. Even as this scenario unfolds, Ms. Martin must first work with the school psychologist to determine the cause of the behavioral outburst, then develop a plan to prevent it from happening for the remainder of the school day. Ms. Martin must ensure she is following the law, as well, by providing this student with as much access as possible to learning with his typically developing peers. In addition to meeting this one student's needs, Ms. Martin still remains responsible for the rest of the students she teaches, whose learning was disrupted because of one student. This creates terrible stress for Ms. Martin, as she feels she is trying to be the "problem-solver" to one student who is clearly in crisis while she is simultaneously "letting down" the other students in the group, who were engaged and learning before the incident occurred.

As difficult as it may seem, this incident is a very typical example of what special education teaching is like in public schools today. While the scene unfolded, were you able to identify with this example? How is it similar or different than what you experience? How might you approach the situation differently? Did you have empathy for the teacher who struggled to meet the needs of all the learners?

When a student is in crisis, the school team responds, as best as it can, in an effort to problem-solve. As you can see in the above scenario, the educational team utilized an elaborate protocol, communicating with and engaging various professionals to meet the needs of one student. This happens multiple times on a daily basis in public schools nationwide. While the educational team works to gather data and determine possible future steps within the school setting, the parent is then contacted to relay important information to the school. After all, there may have been an incident before school that affected the student's behavior. The educational team cannot and should not be the sole decision-maker in student issues. It is therefore necessary for the school and the parent to build a continuum of data that connects home life and school life.

As the parent is contacted, the educational team begins to collaborate and develop a case for the student behavior in question. The parent will then be consulted by the team and any additional evidence will be added to the case. As evidence is collected and analyzed, the team is responsible for communicating the educational implications of the resulting data from the student and the team to the parent. The problem is that the parent may not always understand the implications of the resulting data, because the language is written in a way that the parent is not able to decode or understand due to various cultural or cognitive differences. The parent may also not know what questions to ask the team regarding the legal rights of the child.

The question you should then ask yourself as a teacher is: *"If parents are not aware of or able to understand all of the educational and legal implications of the team decision-making regarding their child, are they truly being given an equal opportunity to share in that decision-making regarding those educational and legal implications?"* This is an incredibly important question, because great school districts can and do provide the necessary legal materials and information to parents and students, but there is a gap between what the parents hear or perceive and what they truly understand about the legal obligations of public schools regarding their child and how they affect the implications for educational instruction. This is not the fault of the public school system, and it is not the fault of the parent. It is simply the consequence of a variety of circumstances, which have resulted in a lack of clear, understandable, and equitable communications developed between the home and the school. Positive communication is truly vital in these circumstances. The complexity of the law and the tremendous diversity of parent knowledge have created a need for advocacy in special education, especially when heated and emotional discussions take place regarding educational decision-making.

We are sure you agree that both teachers and parents want to be respected for their knowledge and opinions. If you review the examples of all the students discussed in this chapter, you will notice that there were valid concerns from both teachers and parents who worked to create a positive, engaging educational climate at home and at school. There is no "right" answer that defends one side; however, there is one "right", and it belongs to the child. Every child in this nation has a right to a free appropriate public education (FAPE). FAPE is guaranteed by the Rehabilitation Act of 1973 and the Individuals with Disabilities Education Act of 2004. For more information on the historical legal landmarks involving education, please revisit Chapter 1.

Special Education Advocates work to be stewards of the law. It is the advocate's job to act as a liaison between the parent and the school on all legal matters regarding public education. Advocates are the important third party in the special education process, because they help the parent(s) learn, understand, and communicate their child's rights and needs under the requirements of special education law to the public schools. Thus, advocates act as mediators between the teacher and the parent(s) to complete the final partnership in the "Rule of Three".

As you can imagine, advocates are not necessarily fighting "against" the school district, but are simply clarifying in various formal and informal settings the state and legal obligations of our public education system to the family. After all, the educator and the school are expected to know and comply with state and federal guidelines. The advocate simply provides a framework for the team to do so in such a way that the process is truly equitable and fair not only to the district, but to the parent and, more importantly, to the child. The beauty of advocacy is that it relieves the pressure of a two-sided situation. It provides clarity. Good teachers know that in a 21st-century learning environment, collaborative teaching, using objective data to drive instruction, is not an individual task, but the task of a team. A team of "experts" is responsible for analyzing, planning, and implementing a child's educational plan. One of the experts in the team of three is the parent. That expertise comes from knowing the child more than any other expert can or ever will.

Shouldn't parents have the right to understand the implications of their contribution to the decision-making team? Shouldn't parents understand all of the educational services their child is entitled to by law – not because the parent isn't an expert on his/her child, but because the parent has the right to participate, according to the law, in how to make the best decision possible? The advocate helps protect the child by empowering the parent with the necessary tools to have an educated and legal voice in the process. After all, if you believe the team is working for the good of the child, then every expert in the team should have all the tools necessary to make the right decision. That is advocacy. That is why the "Rule of Three" works. It serves to empower the entire team to make the best decision possible for the child.

Conclusion

Knowing that a parent has hired an advocate to assist in ensuring that his/her child's needs are being met used to be scary for some teachers. In fairness, in some schools, it still is. It shouldn't be, though. As stated at the beginning of this chapter, advocates are on our side as long as we are on the side of the child with special needs. If we aren't on the child's side, then we may need to revisit our processes. Advocates are paid to be somewhat one-sided. Work with them, not against them.

The same can be said of parents. Whether or not the parent hires an advocate, that parent wants what is best for his/her child. Schools do, too. There is no reason for us to be on opposite sides, since we have the same end goals. Now, some parents are challenging to work with, for a variety of reasons. In Chapter 7 we provide some resources to assist you in cases where parents are difficult.

The "Rule of Three" illustrates the extreme benefits of working together for the benefit of students. Working together may involve conflicts or "bumps in the road". However, it is worth it in the end, when all students with special needs can and do receive the free appropriate public education they deserve.

6

Advocating as a Parent

Throughout this chapter, we focus specifically on how parents can best include themselves and feel valuable as a teacher's best partners. We write this chapter as if we are
speaking directly to parents. If you are an educator reading this book, consider much of
what we have written here as a script. If you are a parent or an advocate, consider this
chapter to be the one that directly speaks to you. Regardless, our expectation is that
this chapter will give you valuable information on how best to partner with teachers.

In Chapter 5, we introduced you to the "Rule of Three", which included the
parent, the teacher, and the advocate. When there are situations where using
an advocate is not possible, then it is even more imperative that a parent or a
teacher advocate for the child. Every child who is in the process of being
evaluated for special education services needs an adult to speak up for his/
her rights to receive the same educational opportunities as his/her typically
developing peers. After all, whether you are a parent or a teacher, we are sure
your goal is to ensure that the child in your care gets the best education
possible.

Becoming a parent advocate is not always a simple process. However, the
easiest way to begin the process of advocating for your child is to build
a relationship with the school team. To do this, you first need to develop a
positive rapport with the teachers, the administrators, and the other school-
related professionals at your child's school. Remember, teachers are not the

enemy. Just like you, they also want what is best for your child. There isn't a teacher we know who went into his/her career with the intent of "getting rich".

 ## Considerations to Ponder

Teachers want to see students succeed. It is a reflection of their dedication to you, your child, and the world in which we all live. Helping kids learn and grow into responsible, caring citizens is what they love to do. That is why they are in that classroom, day after day, teaching your child. There are other careers that pay more, require less work, and offer perks and benefits that teaching in a public school system cannot provide. Teachers choose to teach because they really want to make a difference in the lives of the children they serve. Do all you can to show your child's teacher that you want to be a partner for your child.

Parent–Teacher Partnering Tips

Now that you know how much teachers care, also know that teachers really want to be your partner in educating your child. They need you. They care about you, and they are hoping that someday, your child will do amazing things with his/her life. Most teachers are parents, too. They think of your kids as their kids, and that makes them different from any other profession in the world. As we begin this chapter, Figure 6.1 shows five tips to get the

Figure 6.1 Parent–Teacher Partnering Tips

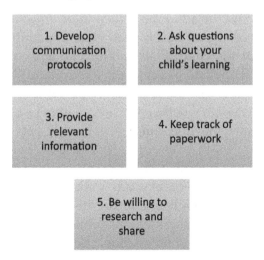

relationship with your child's teacher off to the right start. This will help you as you begin to advocate for your child.

All five of these tips may seem simple to you, but if one or more of them is not implemented, then the ability to build a successful rapport between home and school decreases dramatically. This is important for both parents and teachers when it comes to serving students with a suspected disability, because research shows that when teachers and parents partner together, the likelihood of success for the child is greater. A united front is a powerful front when it comes to advocacy.

Tip #1: Communication Protocol

In today's busy world, communication often seems difficult. There are responsibilities and demands pulling at our time and attention. Thankfully, communication opportunities have evolved with the integration of varying types of technology. Review Chapter 4 on communication to gain a deeper understanding of the communication process and where breakdowns can occur, but for now, this section will give you a basic overview of the types of communication available for parents and teachers today. Teachers and parents have greater resources and more choices than ever before in how to communicate with one another. Think about it: phone, email, text messaging, and interactive applications such as *Bloomz*, *Remind*, and *SimplyCircle* (interactive applications which can be downloaded and installed on a phone or tablet), all create a quick and easy way to stay in touch. The most difficult part of communicating isn't about access or choices, but about effort. It is both important and necessary to stay in touch with your child's teacher, if not on a daily basis, then on a weekly basis. Ask your child's teacher what type of communication system he/she plans to use, how often it will be used, and in what way it will be used. We recommend that you establish a predictable routine on when to communicate, and then agree to review this routine at the end of every grading period to determine whether it was successful or needs adjustment. This may seem like a lot of work at first, but once you get a system in place, you will find that having a predictable way to communicate is the easiest and most effective way to problem-solve if a problem comes about. The whole point of good communication is to avoid misunderstandings and to remain vigilant about your child's needs. That is why this tip is number one. Much like other types of relationships, communication is the key to understanding.

Tip #2: Ask Questions

Once you have established a rapport with the teacher, you need to know what questions to ask. If your childhood was anything like ours, parents rarely asked their child's teacher specific questions about how their child was learning, what goals and content they were working on, and with whom their learning would occur. In fact, the typical question of a 1980s parent may have been: "Is Johnny behaving in school?" Parents during that generation were much more worried about behavior rather than content or delivery of instruction. In the latter part of the 20th century, teachers were seen as authority figures and parents often regarded the teacher's opinion as law. Today, teachers are seen as educational resources and experts in pedagogy, but they aren't seen as the sole decision-maker or the authority figure they once were. Teachers today are expecting parents to engage in their child's teaching and learning process by asking specific questions regarding content, delivery, assessment, and evaluation of their child's goals. Twenty-first-century teachers are trained to use data to drive instruction. When collected and analyzed accurately, the data provides easy answers for parents who have questions. So never be afraid to be specific. Sure, Johnny's teacher will still hope you ask if he is behaving. Just be prepared if you do, because the teacher will pull out a behavior chart that shows you just how many times Johnny was out of his seat to throw away trash and talk to his friend.

Five Great Questions to Ask the Teacher

1. What concepts in math and reading is my child learning this year, and how can I support that learning at home?
2. What ideas do you have for helping my child complete homework?
3. Where can I find educational websites which may help support what my child is learning during the school day?
4. What are my child's greatest strengths?
5. What are my child's greatest challenges?

In addition to those five questions, it never hurts to jot down some questions which are specific to your child's personal situation. *Maybe you want to know how Johnny is getting along with the new kid. Maybe you are wondering why Johnny never eats his lunch.* Any and every question you ask is important. Just be sure to ask them – and don't forget to write down the answers you are given. You may want to ask the same questions (or similar) again after the next grading period. This helps you, as a parent, stay informed. It also helps keep track of what conversations took place, what follow-up was made, and whether or not the issues were resolved. Good recordkeeping is an asset for both parents and teachers, as it prevents miscommunication and misunderstandings later.

Tip #3: Provide Relevant Information

One thing you may learn about your child's teacher is how much he/she values knowing about your child's home life, as it contributes immensely to the educational process. It may be difficult to share deeply personal circumstances, but doing so gives the teacher the opportunity to find and share resources you may want or need. In school settings, guidance counselors often act as liaisons between home and school, providing students and families with community connections needed to make life outside school a little easier. In the story below, you will see an example of how one child's home life was greatly impacted by the team of teachers and staff at an elementary school. The relevant information shared by the family was entrusted to the teaching staff to keep confidential.

At the beginning of his third grade school year, "Mark" was a gentle, bright, and popular student who was known for being kind and friendly toward all members of his class. The teacher often chose Mark to serve as a classroom leader in various capacities throughout the school day. When new students started in Mark's class, he always sat by them, welcoming them with a friendly face and lots of assistance. As the year progressed, Mark became more withdrawn. He stopped offering to do things for other students and wanted to sit by himself at lunch. He was not doing well academically, either. The teacher couldn't find any way to motivate Mark. She began to suspect a learning disability. The sweet little boy lost his bright smile and engaging personality, so she sent him to the guidance counselor and the school psychologist to see what could be done for him.

After the school psychologist and guidance counselor interviewed Mark, they immediately reached out to Mark's mom. The counselor learned in a few short conversations with Mark's mom that Mark's father had become very sick, lost his job, and the family was struggling financially and emotionally. With permission from Mark's mom, the entire school held an ice cream social, which included an opportunity for students and families of the entire district to play games and win prizes. No one knew that the proceeds from the event would go to assist Mark's family except Mark's mom. However, the teachers all knew that Mark was experiencing difficulties at home, so they made sure to give Mark the space he needed to heal from the traumatic change in his home life. No one expected Mark to be the happy, cheery lad he once was. Assignments were allowed to be turned in a little later, and more patience was given to Mark when he just couldn't concentrate or needed to be absent to spend time with his ailing father. The teachers significantly adapted their instructional process to assist Mark when he needed it, but maintained the same curriculum as they had before.

Luckily, by the end of the year, Mark's dad recovered from his illness, his family was able to stay in their home, and Mark was back to his jolly, bright self. The school had rallied together to assist Mark in the most confidential, loving manner, just when he needed it. This story is only one example of why it is important to share relevant information. As a parent, it may be hard to go to the school for help when you need it. However, asking for help from professionals who only want the very best for your child could be the key to building a team of support that makes all the difference in your child's life, both at home and at school. It also proves that Mark did not have a disability. He just needed a different kind of care.

Tip #4: Keep Track of Paperwork

In today's electronic age, it would seem that there would be less written information circulating between home and school. However, that is not the case. The legal and medical information that comes with determining whether a child qualifies for special education services is of greater significance than it has ever been before. That is because educating students with disabilities is an expensive proposition for public schools today. It is vital for both parents and teachers to keep track of any and all official documents which may support the identification process. Later, this helps to determine the best resources possible for the student, and may support the requirement of specific funds to be disbursed to the district for the educational needs of the child. Remember, according to the law, every child is eligible for a free appropriate public education (FAPE). Your tax dollars are hard at work supporting public schools. Having the appropriate documents helps to ensure your child is receiving all the supports and services he/she needs to be educated in his/her least restrictive environment.

The parent is responsible for providing certain types of documents when meetings are convened. Some examples of written documentation to bring to IEP meetings include medical information, custody information, and homework samples. This is just a short list, but an important one. Medical information is by far the most important resource to bring to a meeting. Documentation from outside professionals, such as neurologists or psychiatrists, helps validate what the team or parent may be seeing in observable behavior, both at school and at home. This provides the team with third-party evidence and enables the parent to advocate on the child's behalf to receive the kind of resources the child needs to be educated along with his/her typically developing peers.

Tip #5: Be Willing to Research and Share

There is probably nothing more frustrating or disappointing than hearing bad news about your child. After all, no parent wants to believe his/her child is struggling. We all want the very best for our children: health, happiness, and a chance of being a productive member of society. If you want to convince others that you see value in understanding your child's condition and behaviors, then do a little research to gain background information on your child's struggles, write down what you find, and share your thoughts and suggestions at the meeting. Strong educational teams *always* encourage parent involvement. Remember, teachers become teachers because they want to help students learn. If you come prepared with research and resources that you think may help your child, your thoughts and ideas will not be discounted, but considered valuable in the identification process. As former teachers, we both can reassure you that teaching professionals *need* and *want* your advice when it comes to your child. Bring a notebook to the meeting, share your ideas, and jot down any ideas the team may have. Share your thoughts about what you see, what resources you want and need for your child, and we will work to help you get them. Together, the team will work to create a plan that meets your child's needs, both at home and at school.

Being a parent advocate isn't always this easy. Even though you may have learned a few key strategies, what happens if you need legal advice? What if your child's situation is a bit more complicated? What if the district in which you live claims they have "no more room" for your child in their special education program or no more funds to support your child's educational needs?

If this is the case, then the next section will be of tremendous value to you. Just know that advocating for your child is not a privilege, but a right. You are doing nothing wrong by walking politely and respectfully into a public school and asking for help. It is the job of the public school to assist you, and you need to be prepared with all the relevant information you can bring to support your cause. Parents becoming advocates for their children in public schools is more common than ever before, because state and federally funded programs offer limited resources. The resources are spread fairly thin in order to meet the needs of large numbers of students. This is why many parents must advocate in order for their children to get what they need. It is simply a result of supply and demand.

Advocacy Support

This section will be especially useful if you need legal resources to help you advocate. No need to run to the library or search the Web. These resources are right here, ready for you to use immediately. We suggest you bookmark this page and highlight the most relevant resources you might need to use. Some are national resources, which will enable you to connect with both state and local resources as well (Table 6.1).

When you become an advocate, whether you do it as a professional or as a parent, you must arm yourself with information. The key to successful advocacy is to first know what the law (federal or state) says, then know how to

Table 6.1 Legal Resources for Disability Rights

Agency	Phone	Email/Website
National Information Center for Children and Youth with Disabilities	1-800-695-0284	nichcy@aed.org
Families and Advocates Partnership at PACER Center	1-888-248-0822	www.fape.org
Disability Law Center at the Community Legal Center	1-800-550-4182	www.disabilitylawcenter.org
AG Bell Association's Children's Rights Advocate	1-866-377-5220	info@agbell.org

apply the law. The agencies listed in Table 6.1 will be happy to guide you through the advocacy process, provide important resources, and connect you with the advocacy network in your area. However, it is up to you to take the initiative to learn everything you can, and to be prepared to defend your knowledge. Public school systems receive limited dollars to spend on special education. Many administrators have to limit the amount and type of resources per student in order to manage their fiscal budgets. This isn't something they want to do to restrict funding for a student with special needs; it is something they are required to do by law. Public school districts are held accountable for public funds and how they are distributed. However, remember that it is the child's right to receive all the resources he/she needs to receive FAPE. This means that you may have to provide third-party documentation from other professionals (medical, psychological, etc.) in order to support your cause. Regardless of what you do to prepare for your meeting, remember that the school district and the team of professionals who serve your child are not your enemy. They are here for you. However, their task is not easy. They must be prepared to protect not only the needs of your child, but also the needs of all children they serve. This makes their job especially difficult, because they want to give every child they serve everything he/she needs, but they are only provided with limited resources. They are charged with representing the district in two ways: be fiscally responsible, and be educationally responsive. It is a difficult balance, but an important one.

Always remember that you are the leader in the advocacy process, especially if you are the parent advocating for your child. Have confidence in your ability to speak for your child, and remember that because of you, your child is getting what he/she needs during the school day to be successful. The special education laws were established to protect the rights of the vulnerable. It is to your advantage to know everything you can about your child's rights under the law and to be the voice for your child. Teachers are grateful when parents speak up, because teachers know that parents have the power to get things done. It is also important to remember that when you advocate for your child, you are not only setting a precedent for your child's education, but for the education of other students who may have needs like your child. We believe, as educators, that this is a tremendous bonus to what you are doing, as it has a ripple effect in our public education system. Education is universal. It is important for *every* child to get what he/she needs. The more you do for one, the more you do for all.

Know the Lingo

Advocacy can be challenging when you're unfamiliar with special education lingo. There are so many acronyms associated with 21st-century education today that we've heard people refer to it as "alphabet soup". Even if you are well versed in your knowledge of special education law, you may still want to familiarize yourself with the lingo that teachers, school psychologists, and administrators use to discuss your child's services. This section covers the current key terms in education listed below. We will also use them in context, so that everyone can better understand their meaning and how the words will be used during your meetings. It may be beneficial to highlight key terms, which may help as you converse in your meetings with public school representatives. Not all states use these terms interchangeably, but they are extremely common.

Most Common Acronyms in Special Education

Individualized Education Plan (IEP) – *Johnny's scores provided the evidence the team needed to create an IEP for him.*

Response to Intervention (RtI) – *After Susan did not achieve success in a regular education setting, she was placed on an RtI plan in order to determine if more support would help her.*

Evaluation Team Report (ETR) – *The ETR showed the qualitative and quantitative evidence gathered by the team and the results of the evidence, which proved the student was eligible for an IEP.*

Behavior Intervention Plan (BIP) – *Stephen's behaviors had escalated and had become consistent across multiple environments, so the team decided to implement a BIP.*

Specific learning disability (SLD) – *Rebecca's scores showed that she was of average intelligence, but there was a significant discrepancy in both her math and reading scores, so she was eligible to receive special education services for her SLDs in math and reading.*

Cognitive disability (CD) or intellectual disability (ID) – *The student's ID was evidenced by the significant discrepancy on test scores, demonstrating very low cognitive functions compared to his/her typically developing peers.*

Free appropriate public education (FAPE) – *Every student in the United States has the right to receive FAPE according to federal law.*

Least restrictive environment (LRE) – *A student, once evaluated for special education services, should receive his/her education in the LRE which will meet his/her educational needs.*

A valuable practice might be to continue listening for key terms in your school setting that we have failed to mention or that are unique to your particular state or district. As a service to the school, let teachers know which terms they take for granted that might seem foreign to parents. You can be extremely helpful in helping to keep the lexicon at a level and of a tenor that everybody can be comfortable with.

Conclusion

In recent years, many educators have become inundated with the news stories and popular media posts about "helicopter parents" – parents who hover over the teacher and their child. So much of the information is jaded and designed to make teachers fear and loathe parents. While this occurs, too few teachers are receiving any education or staff development about how to work effectively and collaboratively with parents.

The first step to having a collaborative relationship with parents is to truly believe that all parents want what's best for their children. They may not always know what is educationally best, and your job as an educator is to help them understand things from an educational point of view. When parents are serving in an advocacy role for their children, they are doing so because they need to ensure that their child is receiving the quality education that he/she deserves. It is unnecessary to be threatened by that or to be skeptical in any way. Simply remember that you are the educational expert, and that parents want what's best for their child, just as you do from the teacher's perspective.

7

How to Keep Parent Relationships Positive

In this chapter, we focus on some advice and strategies for working in a collaborative way with parents. While the information is applicable to all school settings, it is important to note the special challenges that are created when parents are trying to advocate for their child who needs special educational attention in the school setting. Teachers are well served to be empathetic, proactive, and positive. By doing so, you will help parents be the collaborative partners their children deserve.

At this point, you have a really solid picture of how special education environments today have come to be. You've read about much of the landmark legal work that created terminology and policies that still persist today. You understand how they gave rise to instructional strategies used today in schools. You have a strong understanding of the Individualized Education Plan (IEP) process, and you understand clearly why communication must be positive and trusting in order to be most effective. Finally, you recognize the valuable role of the teacher, the advocate, and the parent, and you have a great understanding of how the three can and should work together.

Now, we turn our attention to what happens when things don't work well. Despite our best efforts to collaborate, the situations surrounding special education placement decisions, goals, and assessments can bring out emotions and strong feelings, particularly in parents. When that happens, we all need to understand how best to diffuse anger and how to ensure that we demonstrate for parents our strong desire to see them and work with them in partnership.

To say that parents play a significant role in advocating for the needs of their children is akin to stating the obvious. Similarly obvious is the recognition of the trove of information parents have about their children and how they learn. Because of this, teachers should value and appreciate the vital role that parents play in determining what a child's special needs may be and in collaboratively determining how to best meet those needs. In short, parents ought to be viewed as critical members of the team that collaborates to ensure appropriate instruction and learning opportunities for their child. This is why the previous chapter focused exclusively on how parents can best serve as cooperative advocates.

Too often, however, parents are viewed as the enemy. Teachers and administrators in many schools immensely dislike collaborating with parents because some parents are really challenging. After being told that their child is "disabled" and after learning about terms like IEP, many parents become defensive, confrontational, or an unpredictable combination of both.

So how should a teacher deal with this apparent dichotomy? On the one hand, parents are invaluable teammates and the best advocate for their child's needs, while on the other hand, they are challenging to work with. Teachers have enough responsibilities already, as meeting diverse learning needs in an ever-changing educational environment is one of the most difficult occupations one could possibly enter.

Absent from most teacher preparation in higher education today, and as a professional development option in the majority of school districts, are any information, skills, or techniques for working with challenging parents. Yet those teachers who have developed skills to do so are the ones who enjoy the collaboration and insights that only a parent can bring. All teachers need to have these skills and insights, and this chapter will provide important information to get you there.

First, it is essential to understand that at least 90 percent of parents do a good job raising their children and supporting their schools. However, 100 percent of parents do the best job they know how to do. We have to understand that many of their role models did not provide them the examples and structures they need to be effective parents. Oftentimes, we compare our most troubling parents' reactions to the way our own parents would have reacted or the way the other parents in our neighborhood would have reacted. And to be truthful, if you have a positive family structure, many parents do react in that exact same manner today. We have already figured out how to deal with the easy ones; anybody can do that. What takes so much of our time, worry, and energy is the 5 percent of the parents that we often have to deal with the most. It is important to keep a positive perspective regarding the students we work with, and equally important to keep that productive focus when we think of and work with their parents. After all, they are the best parents our students have.

Another thought to keep in mind is analogous to teaching. Consider the fact that the students we typically are most tempted to yell at have probably been treated like that for much of their lives. We need, therefore, to teach these students a new way to interact, not just polish their inappropriate skills. The same thing applies to parents. If we believe they are doing the best they know how, but we still don't find them cooperative, then one of our goals should be to help them to improve. We believe we have a responsibility as educators to consistently model appropriate behaviors for everyone that we come in contact with. And our personal view is that we need to do this *all* of the time. That is, we need to do it ten days out of ten, not just nine out of ten. If you question this and think that the 100 percent standard may be too high, then just ask yourself two questions: "How many days out of ten do I expect the students in my classroom and school to behave themselves?" and "How many days out of ten do I hope that parents treat me with respect and dignity?" If the answer to these questions is ten days out of ten, then we must ensure that we behave professionally on an equal number of days ourselves.

Rule #1

As mentioned in a book Doug wrote with Dr. Todd Whitaker, *Dealing with Difficult Parents* (Whitaker and Fiore, 2016), we should never argue, yell, use sarcasm, or behave unprofessionally with a parent, despite how the parent may be treating us. We all have to remember that advocating for your own child is an experience that is laced with emotions. While the previous chapter provides instructions for parents about how best to advocate, we also know that not all of them will have read this book. As such, it is possible that parents will come to IEP conferences or just show up at the school or classroom irritated, or even irrational. As teachers, both of us have been yelled at by parents. But we never yelled back. Also, we have seen parents behave unprofessionally, and we have experienced efforts from upset parents to drag us into an argument. We never argued, and we never behaved unprofessionally, though.

The key word to remember in this rule is *never*. A challenge we face as educators is that, in our exhaustion, some of us can be baited. We sometimes feel as though we are being forced to argue, when in fact that is never the case. All of us control how many arguments we get in. All of us control our own emotional responses to things that occur. Again, advocating for a child with special needs, whether you're a parent, teacher, or advocate, is an emotional process. When emotions are charged, people often say the wrong thing. Sometimes, they even say the right thing, but they say it in the wrong way. As educators, we need to hold ourselves to a higher standard. Hence, Rule #1. We never argue, yell, use sarcasm, or behave unprofessionally with parents.

As we work to understand things from a parent's point of view and as we hold ourselves to a very high standard of behavior and communication, we must be mindful of the fact that many of the parents we collaborate with did not have positive experiences when they were schoolchildren. In fact, attending school during an era that placed less emphasis on affective education than contemporary schools do, many of these parents do not view schools as places that concern themselves at all with the feelings and attitudes of the students. Also, in light of the many changes that have taken place in regard to the education of children with special needs and the focus on serving these students appropriately, many parents still remember back to the days when schools were not quite so sensitive about different abilities. Remember, laws that protect the learning needs of all children are contemporary. Differentiating instruction is still a new concept when examined across the known history of teaching and learning techniques. Many parents remember all too clearly that the only opinions that really mattered in determining a student's educational goals were those of school personnel. These parents, therefore, are not used to having their opinions count in educational settings. They simply think of school as something negative. The cause of these negative school experiences and feelings is irrelevant. It makes little difference whether parents view school negatively because of their own lack of effort to succeed or because of their perception that school failed them. The importance lies in the fact that the mere mention of the word "school" conjures up negative images for some of our parents. Add these negative feelings to the emotions many parents feel when their children are having trouble in school, and it really makes sense why some parents can present challenges.

Pay Attention to the F Word

The F word is "fair". One of the major concerns that parents have when they do not like the treatment their child is receiving is fairness. When you think about it, all of us are like that to a certain extent. We all want to be treated fairly. We all notice and become concerned when we don't feel we are being treated fairly. A strong sense of fairness and how we are entitled to it resides deep within us all. Therefore, you shouldn't be surprised if a parent accuses you of being unfair. Perhaps they believe that the expectation you have for their child's performance is unfair. Perhaps they feel as though their child's IEP is unfair because it does not call for the same accommodations as the IEP of a classmate. Fairness matters.

When we think back to the regulatory environment and the court cases that helped define special education services today, one of the hallmark terms and concepts to emerge has been a free appropriate public education (FAPE). We'll bet you remember what that stands for. When we think of the right all children have to FAPE, fairness is implied. If the education a child receives is not appropriate for him/her and his/her abilities, of course it will be viewed by the parents as being unfair.

When parents use the F word with us, we need to help them understand what fairness really means. We need to do this in a positive, non-threatening, yet confident way. Consider the following situation as an example.

Let's say that a parent raises a concern about fairness during an IEP meeting. The parent in this example believes that the behavior modification plan designed for her child is inappropriate and fails to provide enough room for her child to have a bad day. The parent states:

> It's not fair that Ricky is only allowed to speak out of turn twice, or he doesn't get a gold star on the letter I sign. He loves those gold stars, and we reward him at home when one is on the note. On the days where he fails to get one, he's depressed. It's just not fair.

One way to reply would be to acknowledge the parent's concern about fairness. If we are defensive or dismissive, then the situation may get worse. So you could say something like:

> Mrs. Harrigan, I can tell that you care about Ricky and you care about fairness, and I want you to know that I do, too. What wouldn't be fair would be if I let Ricky have a gold star even if he spoke out of turn three or four times. It wouldn't be fair because we all determined during our last IEP conference that Ricky has the ability to control his impulses better than that. I would not be giving Ricky a fair chance to develop the skills necessary for success in this world, even though all of us, you included, believe he is capable of developing them. I love how motivational the gold stars are for Ricky, and I am so grateful that I can count on you to reinforce this plan at home so that Ricky works even harder to earn them.

A couple of important words and phrases are contained in your response. First, you used the word "fair" repeatedly. This helps the parent redefine and reconceptualize the term in her own mind. It helps her see that being fair does not mean the same thing as giving in, or turning a blind eye. This is very important.

Second, you are thanking and validating the parent. While thanking her, you are pointing out the assistance and collaboration that you would appreciate. The last sentence in your response informs the parent in a completely non-threatening way that her cooperation and reinforcement at home will make things better for Ricky. Do we have any doubt that she, like us, wants anything other than what's best for him?

The F word can be useful to us if we use it mostly in response to parents who use it with us. More important than the words we use, though, is the manner in which we say them. Responses to parent or advocate concerns must be delivered in a caring and non-threatening manner.

The Importance of Being Proactive

Whether or not we are preparing for an IEP meeting, a parent–teacher conference, or any other formal meetings with parents or advocates, as educators we need to always be proactively communicating when there are problems. It is very frustrating to parents if they attend a meeting and learn that their child has been having a problem for a long time. If a teacher explains a struggle or a problem that has been persisting with a student, parents are very likely to ask why they didn't know about the problem earlier. As a result of that question, the teacher may feel defensive. Typically, when we feel defensive, it is because we did something wrong. Proactively communicating with parents before problems persist prevents these defensive feelings.

Another way to be proactive with parents is to take advantage of the numerous opportunities all schools have for breaking down barriers. We have both worked in schools that hosted fun fairs, academic fairs, and field day activities which required parents and teachers to work side by side. The equalization of these two distinct roles that came about as a result of these activities was, in all cases, positive. Parents saw teachers in a new light, and teachers saw a very cooperative, caring side of parents. Perhaps more importantly, students enjoyed seeing their parents working with their teachers. This enjoyment is not unique to the special needs population. However, as the nature of advocacy typically is more important for parents whose children have special learning needs, it is vital that we work to involve those parents in these activities.

It's a fact of life that most people enjoy introducing people they respect and admire to one another. We can recall many instances in which a respected colleague, supervisor, or teacher was introduced to one of our family members. It brought us great joy to have these two people, whom we admired and respected, meet each other for the first time. Think, for a moment, about elementary school open houses and parent–teacher conferences. While some students fear what might be said at those conferences, even those kids love the idea that their parents will meet and get to know their teacher, and vice versa.

So take advantage of these opportunities, and consider their importance in building relationships. Throughout this book, we discuss the importance of collaboration, whether from the perspective of an educator, a parent, or an advocate. Aside from the formal opportunities for these collaborations, never forget the myriad other opportunities schools have to create events that build these relationships. Strong relationships lead to strong collaborations.

Parent Involvement at School and at Home

Instinctively, we all know that parent involvement is important. We know that student achievement improves when parents are involved in their education. This may be even more important with parents of students with special needs. We absolutely need the involvement of those parents. As we already have illustrated, teacher, parent, and advocate must work as a team.

Obviously, an organization that greatly supports parent involvement in our schools is the National PTA. In addition to writing several position statements and resolutions about school–parent partnerships, the organization has asked that accredited teacher preparation programs in colleges and universities include in their curricula lessons about how to improve these valuable collaborations. In their *National Standards for Family-School Partnerships* (www. pta.org/nationalstandards), they offer the following six standards for all teachers and schools to employ in their daily practice:

Standard 1: Welcoming all families into the school community – Families are active participants in the life of the school, and feel welcomed, valued, and connected to each other, to school staff, and to what students are learning and doing in class

Standard 2: Communicating effectively – Families and school staff engage in regular, two-way, meaningful communication about student learning.

Standard 3: Supporting student success – Families and school staff continuously collaborate to support students' learning and healthy development both at home and at school, and have regular opportunities to strengthen their knowledge and skills to do so effectively.

Standard 4: Speaking up for every child – Families are empowered to be advocates for their own and other children, to ensure that students are treated fairly and have access to learning opportunities that will support their success.

Standard 5: Sharing power – Families and school staff are equal partners in decisions that affect children and families and together inform, influence, and create policies, practices, and programs.

Standard 6: Collaborating with community – Families and school staff collaborate with community members to connect students, families, and staff to expanded learning opportunities, community services, and civic participation.

In these six standards, there are clear indicators of much of what already has been presented in this book. For example, Standard 4 specifically references advocacy. Standard 5 references the equal partnership between families and school staff. The "Rule of Three" and even some of the special education case law we presented in Chapter 1 are applicable there. The six standards are not only logical and somewhat intuitive, but they have a research-based foundation. Many scholars have studied the effects of parental involvement for decades. Similarly, scholars have studied the impact that positive relationships between parents and teachers can have on the academic achievement of children. The research all has been clear. When parents are involved in their child's schooling, when they have favorable opinions of teachers, and when they believe that their input is considered valuable, the achievement of their children increases.

Considerations to Ponder

Finally, we offer some advice that can be presented to all parents from either a teacher or the school administration. While this advice targets all parents, the presented examples can be even more pertinent to parents of students with special needs. Parents have the power to set the stage for learning in everyday activities at home. Here are some examples of ideas that parents can use to best assist in their child's education from their homes:

- ◆ Set a good example by reading.
- ◆ Read to your children, even after they can read independently.
- ◆ Set aside a family reading time. Take turns reading aloud to each other.
- ◆ Take your children to the library regularly. Let them see you checking out books for yourself, too.

- ◆ Build math and reasoning skills together. Have young children help sort laundry, measure ingredients for a recipe, or keep track of rainfall for watering the lawn.
- ◆ Regulate the amount and content of the television your family watches. Read the weekly TV listing together and plan shows to watch. Monitor the time and use of video game systems.
- ◆ Ask specific questions about school. Show your children that school is important to you, so that it will be important to them.
- ◆ Help your children manage time. Make a chart showing when chores need to be done and when assignments are due.
- ◆ Come to an agreement with each of your children on a regular time and place for homework.
- ◆ Try to schedule homework time for when you or your children's caregiver can supervise.
- ◆ Make sure your children understand their assignments.
- ◆ Follow up on assignments by asking to see your children's homework after it has been returned by the teacher. Look at the teacher's comments to see if your children have done the assignment correctly.
- ◆ Don't do your children's homework. Make sure they understand that homework is their responsibility.

There are many proven techniques for working with parents who are difficult, angry, and frustrating. The purpose of this chapter is not to cover all of those strategies, but to help you understand how easy it is to celebrate what parents already do collaboratively and to educate them on the best ways to be a support for their child. Those of us who are parents understand what a challenging job parenting is. We need also to understand that the typical challenges of parenthood are exacerbated in many instances where a child is receiving special school services under an IEP. Rather than focusing on all of the strategies to use when you are having a difficult time with parents, the outcome we are hoping for here is that you will feel prepared to offer parents friendly advice about how they can help be part of the educational solutions for their children. Finally, it also is of tremendous value for you to recognize that a positive demeanor and an open, proactive approach to potential problems help all teachers tremendously in their work with parents.

Conclusion

Partnerships involve equal work from two or more parties. Challenges arise when one party doesn't wish to do his/her fair share or work hard enough.

Our premise all along has been that we, as educators, must recognize and expect the value that comes from parents and/or advocates. Educating all children is a challenging yet noble task. As any teacher can tell you, doing so alone is much more challenging than doing so as part of a team.

So what can we do when parents and/or advocates don't do their fair share or are difficult to work with? The skills required to remain positive, proactive, sincere, and approachable are skills that we already possess. We simply need the willingness to utilize these skills. We need to recognize that using these skills will lead to collaborative participation which, in turn, will lead to a successful educational experience for children. If we have done our job in writing this book, then you will do everything within your power to engage parents and advocates in the educational process of their children with special needs.

Afterword

There have been students with special needs for as long as there have been children. Although our public schools were set up to educate students based on their perceived needs, for centuries this was done in a one size fits all model. While there always were excellent teachers who tutored or provided extra help to their students who were struggling, formal deliberate programs for meeting the needs of individual learners are still relatively young in the life of education.

There also have always been parents and other adults who were concerned with the education children were receiving. While they rarely were involved in the educational process during this country's first two centuries, parents and other adults did, indeed, always care.

As we have finally reached a point at which serious efforts are made to serve all children, parents have become more active and the concept of an advocate has been born. Children with special learning needs now are identified, and individualized plans are created to help these children have equal access to education. Parents and advocates are essential adults in the equation, as we strive to provide every child with a free appropriate public education.

We wrote this book to assist you in collaborating with parents and advocates. We know that strong communication skills, a good understanding of special education practices and models, and a desire to utilize all of the assistance one can bring to bear to help children with special needs always help students and their families. It is our sincere hope that you found the advice, counsel, and examples presented in this book to be valuable. Remember, we are your partners on this journey.

References

Fiore, D.J. (2016). *School community relations*, 4th ed. New York: Routledge.

Rose, D. (2014, June 18). Learning by Universal Design [Interview with Anthony Rebora]. Retrieved from www.edweek.org/tm/articles/2014/06/18/gp_rose_interview.html.

Vygotsky, L. (1962). *Thought and language*. Cambridge, MA: MIT Press.

Ward, V.S. (1961). *Finding the gifted: An axiomatic approach*. Columbus, OH: Charles E. Merrill.

Whitaker, T.C. and Fiore, D.J. (2016). *Dealing with difficult parents*, 2nd ed. New York: Routledge.

Appendix
About the Individuals with Disabilities Education Act (IDEA)

The material below is excerpted from the US Department of Education website (https://sites.ed.gov/idea/about-idea/).

About IDEA

The Individuals with Disabilities Education Act (IDEA) is a law that makes available a free appropriate public education to eligible children with disabilities throughout the nation and ensures special education and related services to those children.

The IDEA governs how states and public agencies provide early intervention, special education, and related services to more than 6.5 million eligible infants, toddlers, children, and youth with disabilities.

Infants and toddlers, birth through age two, with disabilities and their families receive early intervention services under IDEA Part C. Children and youth ages three through 21 receive special education and related services under IDEA Part B.

Additionally, the IDEA authorizes:

◆ Formula grants to states to support special education and related services and early intervention services.
◆ Discretionary grants to state educational agencies, institutions of higher education, and other nonprofit organizations to support research, demonstrations, technical assistance and dissemination, technology development, personnel preparation and development, and parent-training and -information centers.

Congress reauthorized the IDEA in 2004 and most recently amended the IDEA through Public Law 114–95, the Every Student Succeeds Act, in December 2015.

In the law, Congress states:

Disability is a natural part of the human experience and in no way diminishes the right of individuals to participate in or contribute to society. Improving educational results for children with disabilities is an essential element of our national policy of ensuring equality of opportunity, full participation, independent living, and economic self-sufficiency for individuals with disabilities.

History of the IDEA

On November 29, 1975, President Gerald Ford signed into law the Education for All Handicapped Children Act (Public Law 94–142), now known as the Individuals with Disabilities Education Act (IDEA). In adopting this landmark civil rights measure, Congress opened public school doors for millions of children with disabilities and laid the foundation of the country's commitment to ensuring that children with disabilities have opportunities to develop their talents, share their gifts, and contribute to their communities.

The law guaranteed access to a free appropriate public education (FAPE) in the least restrictive environment (LRE) to every child with a disability. Subsequent amendments, as reflected in the IDEA, have led to an increased emphasis on access to the general education curriculum, the provision of services for young children from birth through five, transition planning, and accountability for the achievement of students with disabilities. The IDEA upholds and protects the rights of infants, toddlers, children, and youth with disabilities and their families.

In the last 40+ years, we have advanced our expectations for all children, including children with disabilities. Classrooms have become more inclusive and the future of children with disabilities is brighter. Significant progress has been made toward protecting the rights of, meeting the individual needs of, and improving educational results and outcomes for infants, toddlers, children, and youths with disabilities.

Since 1975, we have progressed from excluding nearly 1.8 million children with disabilities from public schools to providing more than 6.9 million children with disabilities special education and related services designed to meet their individual needs.

Today, more than 62 percent of children with disabilities are in general education classrooms 80 percent or more of their school day, and early intervention services are being provided to more than 340,000 infants and toddlers with disabilities and their families.

IDEA Resources for Teachers, Parents, and Advocates

The material below is excerpted from the National Educational Association website (www.nea.org/tools/special-education-IDEA-resources.html).

Books Recommended by the National Education Association

MEETING THE CHALLENGE: SPECIAL EDUCATION TOOLS THAT WORK FOR ALL KIDS

By Patti Ralabate

General and special educators alike will find effective strategies to help students struggling to overcome academic or behavior difficulties. This book is filled with useful ideas and practical, timesaving strategies, as well as sample checklists, rubrics, conference planning sheets, and other resources teachers can copy and use or modify to make their own. (2002) 160 pp. Available from NEA's Professional Library.

MY FUTURE, MY PLAN: A TRANSITION PLANNING RESOURCE FOR LIFE AFTER HIGH SCHOOL FOR STUDENTS WITH DISABILITIES AND THEIR FAMILIES

By Dana Sheets and Ed Gold

Helping students with disabilities plan for life after high school is an awesome responsibility. With this set of resources, educators can encourage early, student-centered transition planning for students with disabilities and their families. The set includes the book, teacher's guide, and video—all available in English and Spanish. (2004) Available from NEA's Professional Library.

Websites Recommended by the National Education Association

ABILITY HUB [http://abilityhub.org/]

Assistive technology FAQs and links for people with a disability who find operating a computer difficult, maybe even impossible. This website will direct you to adaptive equipment and alternative methods available for accessing computers.

COUNCIL FOR EXCEPTIONAL CHILDREN [www.cec.sped.org/]

The Council for Exceptional Children (CEC) is the largest international professional organization dedicated to improving educational outcomes for individuals with exceptionalities, students with disabilities, and/or the gifted.

INTERNET RESOURCES FOR SPECIAL CHILDREN [http:// orsaminore.dreamhosters.com/handy/links/uk_various.html]
The IRSC website provides a central starting point that integrates information, resources, and communication opportunities for family, educators, and medical professionals. The directory is organized, comprehensive, and very user-friendly.

LD ONLINE [www.ldonline.org/]
LD Online is the leading information service in the field of learning disabilities, serving more than 200,000 parents, teachers, and other professionals each month.

SCHWAB FOUNDATION FOR LEARNING [www.schwab foundation.org/About-CHSF/Publications/Schwab-Learning.aspx]
Schwab Learning, also affiliated with Charles Schwab, the brokerage firm, offers resources for educators and parents to use in working with kids with learning disabilities. Content on the site includes in-depth information on identifying learning difficulties, managing school and learning, and connecting with others, as well as other resources and publications. The site includes an interactive database to locate Assistive Technology tools for kids with specific needs. Information on this website is also available in Spanish.

TRANSITION TOOLKIT FOR HIGH SCHOOL TEACHERS [www.livebinders.com/play/play/409374]
This website offers information to help teachers identify what youth need to succeed in postsecondary education and adult life. The site has information on schooling, career preparatory experiences, youth development and leadership, and connecting activities.

There are scores of other websites and books that may be of value in understanding and interpreting the IDEA. The important thing is to remember that there are resources to help decode this law. All teachers – special education or general education – parents, advocates, and administrators need access to these.